ORTHO'S All About

Plumbing
Basics

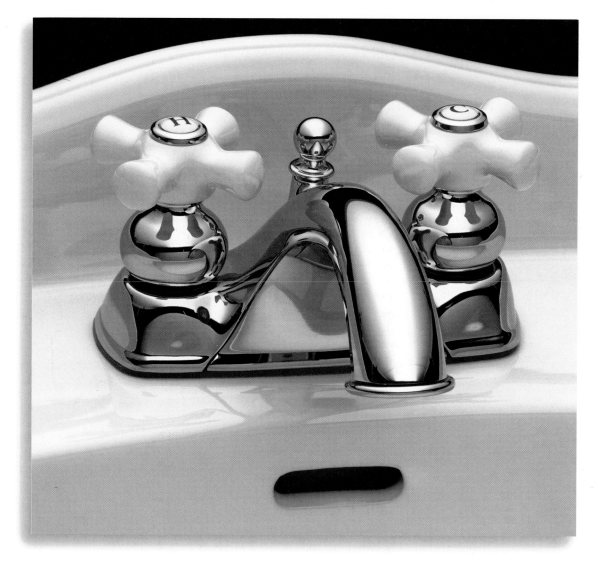

Meredith® Books
Des Moines, Iowa

Ortho® Books
An imprint of Meredith® Books

Ortho's All About Plumbing Basics
Editor: Larry Erickson
Art Director: Tom Wegner
Copy Chief: Catherine Hamrick
Copy and Production Editor: Terri Fredrickson
Contributing Copy Editor: Martin Miller
Technical Reviewer: Ralph Selzer
Contributing Proofreaders: Kathy Eastman, Mary Pas,
    Margaret Smith
Indexer: Nan Badgett
Electronic Production Coordinator: Paula Forest
Editorial and Design Assistants: Kathleen Stevens,
    Karen Schirm
Contributing Editorial Assistants: Janet Anderson,
    Colleen Johnson
Production Director: Douglas M. Johnston
Book Production Managers: Pam Kvitne,
    Marjorie J. Schenkelberg

**Additional Editorial Contributions from
    Greenleaf Publishing**
Publishing Director: Dave Toht
Associate Editor: Steve Cory
Assistant Editor: Rebecca JonMichaels
Editorial Art Director: Jean DeVaty
Design: Melanie Lawson Design
Illustrators: Tony Davis, Lineworks, Tom Mattix,
    Pamela Wattenmaker
Additional Photography: Dan Stultz
Technical Consultant: Michael Clark

Meredith® Books
Editor in Chief: James D. Blume
Design Director: Matt Strelecki
Managing Editor: Gregory H. Kayko

Director, Sales & Marketing, Retail: Michael A. Peterson
Director, Sales & Marketing, Special Markets:
    Rita McMullen
Director, Sales & Marketing, Home & Garden Center
    Channel: Ray Wolf
Director, Operations: George A. Susral

Vice President, General Manager: Jamie L. Martin

Meredith Publishing Group
President, Publishing Group: Christopher M. Little
Vice President, Consumer Marketing & Development:
    Hal Oringer

Meredith Corporation
Chairman and Chief Executive Officer: William T. Kerr

Chairman of the Executive Committee: E.T. Meredith III

Photographers
(Photographers credited may retain copyright ©
    to the listed photographs.)
John North Holtorf: Cover
Dan Stultz: 4-5, 7, 11, 12, 13, 14, 15, 18, 20, 26-27, 28
    (top), 31 (TL), 32 (TR), 33 (TR), 35 (TR), 38-39, 40
    (TR), 42 (TR), 44 (TR), 46 (TR), 50 (TR), 51 (TR), 54
    (TR), 56, 60 (BR), 64 (TR), 66-67, 68 (bottom), 73
    (bottom), 76 (TR), 84-85, 91 (TR), 93 (TL)

All of us at Ortho® Books are dedicated to providing you
with the information and ideas you need to enhance your
home and garden. We welcome your comments and
suggestions about this book. Write to us at:
    Meredith Corporation
    Ortho Books
    1716 Locust St.
    Des Moines, IA 50309–3023

If you would like more information on other Ortho
products, call 800-225-2883 or visit us at www.ortho.com

Note to the Readers: Due to differing conditions, tools,
and individual skills, Meredith Corporation assumes no
responsibility for any damages, injuries suffered, or losses
incurred as a result of following the information published
in this book. Before beginning any project, review the
instructions carefully, and if any doubts or questions remain,
consult local experts or authorities. Because codes and
regulations vary greatly, you always should check with
authorities to ensure that your project complies with all
applicable local codes and regulations. Always read and
observe all of the safety precautions provided by
manufacturers of any tools, equipment, or supplies,
and follow all accepted safety procedures.

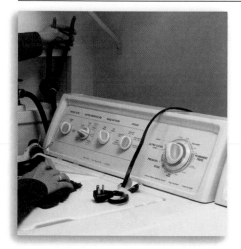

PLUMBING SYSTEMS 4

SKILLS & TOOLS 14

MAINTAINING PIPES 26

COMMON REPAIRS 38

PLUMBING APPLIANCES 66

EXPANDING YOUR SERVICE 84

The word plumbing has a long history, going back to the Latin word for lead. That's because water and waste pipes used to be made of lead—because it was durable. Not anymore. Today's materials are even longer-lasting (and safer) than lead, including PVC plastics for drain and waste lines and rigid copper for supply lines.

PLUMBING SYSTEMS

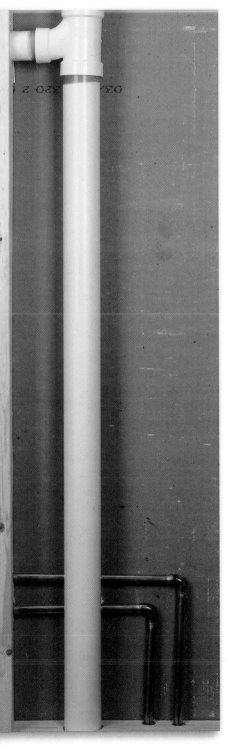

Many people consider plumbing too difficult to tackle themselves. Not only does the work seem grimy and technically difficult, there is always the concern that a do-it-yourself installation will spring a leak. Consequently, most homeowners spend large sums to have someone else perform even simple repairs and installations. Yet, more than any other do-it-yourself skill, plumbing can save you major money.

To accomplish plumbing tasks successfully, you will need to have a general idea of how plumbing systems work and get acquainted with the layout of the plumbing in your own home. Once you understand some basic principles and learn some essential skills, you can install pipes and fixtures that will work as well and last as long as those installed by a licensed plumber. Of course, for a large or complicated job, it might make sense to hire a professional. This book will help you assess your skills so you can decide which jobs you can do yourself. Should you choose to hire a pro, it will equip you to understand the job and to evaluate whether you are getting your money's worth.

This chapter explains the mysteries of water supply, venting, and drainage—all those things that happen behind walls. You'll find that the logic of plumbing is simple, and you'll quickly grasp how to plan any project you undertake.

We'll also help you decide whether elements of your system are improperly installed or outdated. You can do much of the diagnosis yourself. But if you don't understand a part of your plumbing and suspect it may be wrong, call in a professional.

PLUMBING CODES

This book recommends techniques and materials that satisfy the Uniform Plumbing Code for the United States. However, local codes often exceed standards set by the national code. If you are adding new service, contact your local building department to check its requirements and to schedule an inspection, if necessary. (Usually, if you are replacing one fixture with another and will leave the pipes in place, you won't need an inspection.)

Before you call, educate yourself; a building inspector's job is to inspect, not to help you plan. Present a clear diagram of your proposed work and a complete list of the materials you will use. Don't cover up any pipes that need to be inspected until the inspector approves your installation.

THE SUPPLY SYSTEM

I s it safe? That's the first—and most important question about your water supply. If your water comes from a community source, the city or county is responsible for maintaining its purity. If you pump your own, the responsibility is yours.

After that, you'll want to know about how it gets to the various fixtures in your home, how much pressure it should have, and how to shut it off if you need to.

Water comes to your house through a main line from your community or private well. After entering the house, it splits into hot and cold lines connected to your fixtures and appliances.

GO WITH THE FLOW

Water gets to your house through a supply line from a community water system or your private well. In municipal systems, the line first runs through a valve (called a buffalo box or stop box). This is the water supplier's control over your water supply, and it's located outside, usually in the parking strip along the street or somewhere on the property line. In a well system, the supply line brings the water to a pressure tank.

MAIN SHUTOFF: Inside the house (in some cases, outside) the line goes through a main shutoff valve—which gives you control over your water supply—and then diverts for outside faucets.

WATER METER: Next, in most homes water flows through a meter that records the number of gallons used. The exceptions are homes served by private wells and communities that charge a flat water-use fee.

WATER SOFTENER AND WATER HEATER: In hard-water regions that require softening, the supply line goes first to a water softener and then branches again—one line to the water heater and the other (for cold water) bypassing it.

FIXTURES AND APPLIANCES: From there, hot and cold water lines run parallel to each other toward the various fixtures and

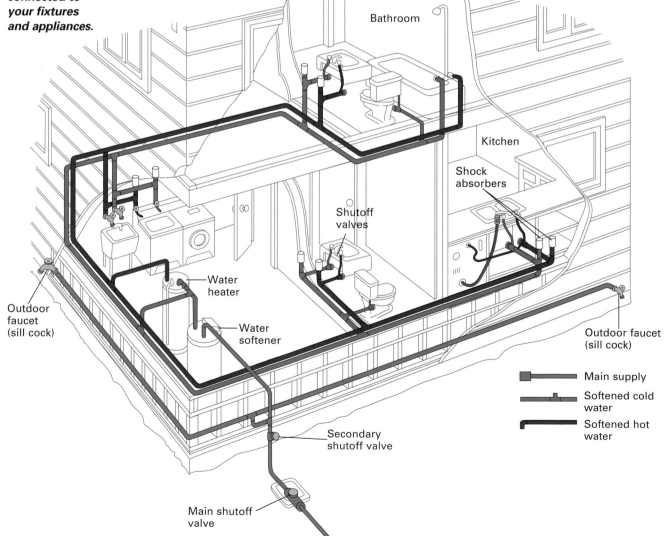

Bathroom

Kitchen

Shock absorbers

Shutoff valves

Outdoor faucet (sill cock)

Water heater

Water softener

Outdoor faucet (sill cock)

Secondary shutoff valve

Main shutoff valve

Main supply

Softened cold water

Softened hot water

appliances in your house—with two exceptions: Dishwashers use hot water only, and toilets use cold. In newer or updated systems, you may have shock absorbers at the faucets—they keep water from "hammering" as it's released from the faucet. At the fixtures, hot is on the left and cold on the right.

WATER-LINE SIZES

Inside the house, the main supply line is ¾- or 1-inch pipe—¾-inch being typical for water heaters and lines feeding more than one fixture. Other lines (except water softener lines in some cities) usually are ½-inch.

WATER PRESSURE

With nothing to obstruct it, water should be delivered at the house at a "street pressure" of 40–55 pounds per square inch (PSI). A low of 20 PSI is acceptable, but a pressure of more than 85 PSI can cause damage. Here's a rough test: Open the faucet nearest the main line's point of entry; if the pressure seems low or high, contact your water supplier.

SHUTOFF

Any time you make repairs to an existing installation or put in a new one, you must shut off the water. Unless a water line is shut off, it is under constant pressure. If you cut a pipe or take a fixture apart without shutting off the water at a point prior to the opening, everything is going to get very wet, and you can't stop the pressure with your hand. Every family member should know how to shut off the water—which you can do at three places. We'll start with the valve closest to the fixture and work our way out to the street.
STOP VALVES: Newer homes have stop valves (shutoff valves) for every fixture and appliance. These let you make a repair without shutting water off and draining the lines for the whole house. Install stop valves whenever the opportunity arises.
MAIN SHUTOFF: You'll find the main shutoff valve for the house near the water meter, or at the point of the pipe's entry. In areas with warm climates, it may be outside, but usually it is just inside the house. If there is a valve before and after the meter, either will do the job. Label the main valve clearly and keep access to it free; do not pile boxes around it. You may need to get to it quickly.

Water meter
Electrical ground
Main shutoff valve

BUFFALO BOX: Sometimes main shutoff valves go bad or the outside water lines break. If the valve inside your house is stuck, or if you have water gurgling up on your lawn, you'll have to shut off the water at the supply valve—the buffalo or stop box. Look in the parking strip along the street or somewhere on the property line.

What you want to find is a metal cover of some sort, which may or may not have the word water on it. You may be able to simply pry it up, or it may be attached with bolts. Contact your water supplier if you are not sure or if you can't get access to the part of the valve that turns it off.

Be aware not only of where the valve is and how to remove its cover but also how to turn the water off. There may be a standard grip that you turn by hand, or you may need a special long-handled "key" that your water supplier may lend you. Often, suppliers prefer to shut off and turn on this valve themselves.
DRAIN THE LINE: Shutting off the water does not remove water that already is in the pipes. Water will continue to run after the shutoff valve has been cranked shut. The lower the outlet, the more water will come out. Before you begin repairs, open the fixtures below (or before) the one you're working on.

Look for the main shutoff valve where the water supply enters your house. Your water meter is attached behind it; sometimes an electrical ground is attached to this pipe. Don't remove this ground; it helps keep your house electrically safe.

Often found in the parking strip, an outdoor shutoff, also referred to as a buffalo box or stop box, is buried so the valve parts are beneath the frost line.

Valve parts

THE DRAIN-WASTE-VENT SYSTEM

Water that comes in must have a way to get out, and that's the function of the drain-waste-vent (DWV) system. Drainpipes carry liquid waste out of the house and into a septic tank or your municipal sewage system. Vent pipes carry sewer gases up and out, and let air in so drains can flow freely. Here's how they work.

BRANCH DRAINS

Water leaving a sink or other fixture enters a curved section of pipe called a trap. Traps are shaped like an **S** or **P** and hold water, which makes a seal to keep gases from backing up into the house. Toilets have built-in traps.

From the trap, water flows through a branch drain line as gravity carries waste out of the house. Drainpipes must slope at least ¼ inch per running foot. When they turn, long-curve elbows help the waste water flow more smoothly. Fixtures require different sizes. Bathroom sink drainpipes are 1¼ inch in diameter; kitchen sinks use 1½-inch lines; and toilets need 3- or 4-inch pipes.

All the branch drain lines tie into a main soil stack, a large-diameter vertical pipe that leads down to the main drain and up through the roof to the main vent stack.

Older homes have cast iron for soil stacks and galvanized steel pipe for drainpipes. Cast iron is very durable, but steel pipes corrode over time. Plastic and copper drain lines are virtually maintenance-free.

Because drain lines sometimes get clogged, look for cleanouts—most systems have them. They're fittings you can open (with a large wrench) so you can insert an auger to clear out the pipes. You can also disassemble traps to provide a point of entry for an auger.

THE MAIN DRAIN

Branch drain lines lead to the main drain, called the house sewer, once it is outside the foundation. It goes to a public sewer line or a septic tank.

The main drain has an inside diameter (ID) of about 4 inches. Depending on when it was installed, it will be made of vitrified clay, cast iron, plastic, or bituminized fiber. Thirsty tree roots like house sewer lines—especially those made of clay and especially in the middle of a dry summer when trees are starved for water. Their fine filaments can work their way into cracks in the line. That is why an older home may need its main drain cleaned out every few years, using a heavy-duty auger that grinds up organic matter.

Generally, all the pipe on your side of the property line is your responsibility; repairs to the sewer line on the street side should be paid, at least in part, by the municipality.

VENT PIPES

For drain water to flow freely, it must have air. Without it, waste water will glug and sputter. Drain lines get their air from main or secondary vent stacks—vertical lines that extend the main or secondary soil stacks up and through the roof. Note in the illustration, *opposite*, how each fixture has not only a branch drain line but also a vent line.

Vents also allow air pressure from above to keep sewer gases from breaking the water seal in the trap. An unvented line may carry water and gases through the fixtures and into the house. That's why venting requirements are so strict. When planning for new service, first figure out how it will be vented.

If your drains are sluggish or gurgle even after augering, you may have a blocked vent pipe or substandard plumbing: The vent may be misused as a drain line for a fixture that needs its own vent.

WHERE DOES THE KITCHEN GREASE GO?

Even if you try to limit your use of grease when you cook, an amazing amount of fatty substance gets poured down your kitchen sink. After several decades, it can build up, clinging to the sides of drainpipes and creating a serious blockage problem.

That's why the kitchen sink in many homes has its own soil stack (usually smaller in diameter than the main soil stack) that goes through a catch basin—a grease trap— on its way to the main stack.

To find your catch basin, look for a large metal cover, perhaps in your backyard near the house. It may be covered by soil and grass, since it typically only needs to be opened every 25 years or so.

Hire a professional pipe-rodding company to scoop the grease out, or purchase a special tool, which looks like a very large ladle, from a plumbing-supply house and scoop it out yourself. Contact your local sanitation department to find the best way to dispose of accumulated grease.

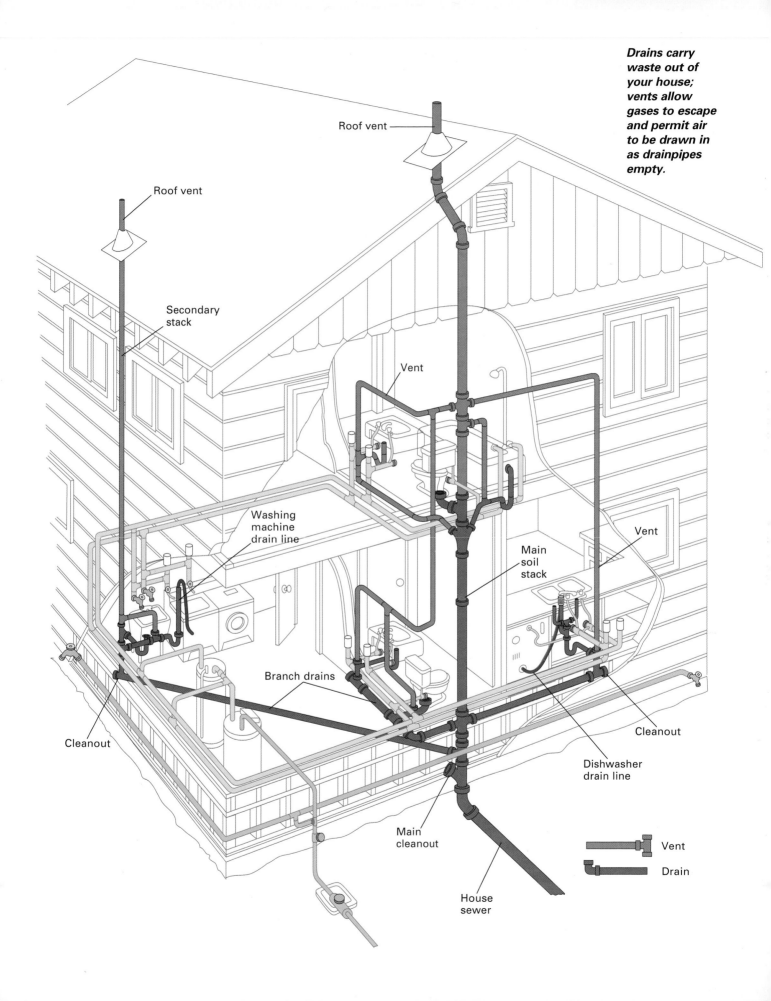

Roof vent

*Drains carry
waste out of
your house;
vents allow
gases to escape
and permit air
to be drawn in
as drainpipes
empty.*

Roof vent

Secondary
stack

Vent

Vent

Main
soil
stack

Washing
machine
drain line

Cleanout

Branch drains

Cleanout

Dishwasher
drain line

Cleanout

Main
cleanout

House
sewer

Vent

Drain

PIPES

If you're working in an older house, you may run into all kinds of pipe material. You probably won't see much leftover lead pipe these days, but you may run into cast iron and galvanized steel.

And although you may end up using cast iron and galvanized steel (*see pages 22–25*), most of your replacement pipe will be copper or PVC (polyvinyl chloride) plastic.

With practice, you can install these materials as securely as a professional can. (*See pages 18–21 for installation techniques.*)

PIPE SIZES

Professionals can tell a pipe's size by looking at it, but it's a little tricky for the beginner. Different standards are used for different pipe. For example, rigid copper is designated by its inside diameter (ID), soft copper by its outside diameter (OD). Schedule 40 PVC is sized by ID, other PVC is designated by its OD. Galvanized steel is measured by ID but these measurements are rounded. A ¼-inch nipple will measure closer to ⅜-inch ID and a ⅜-inch closer to ½ inch.

When measuring the length of a pipe, include the socket depth—the distance a pipe will screw into a fitting.

Keeping it all straight can have even a determined do-it-yourself plumber feeling drained. Sometimes the simplest solution is hard to beat: If you need to replace a pipe, take a piece of the old one with you when you buy the replacement. There is no shame and little chance of error in announcing simply, "I need one of these, without the leak."

If that isn't possible, take measurements with inexpensive calipers and tell the dealer what kind of pipe you've measured. The dealer will know what you need.

Remember, the first goal is no leaks; but a close second is no return trips to the store to exchange stuff you bought by mistake.

To determine the inside diameter of a pipe, first measure the circumference with a piece of masking tape and divide by 3.14. The result is the outside diameter. Then subtract the thickness of the pipe.

LEAD PIPE AND JOINTS

Roman ruins thousands of years old contain lead pipes and lead-soldered joints that look like they were installed yesterday. In many ways, lead is the ideal material for pipes:
■ It lasts for millennia.
■ Its low melting point eases the job of making pipe joints.
■ And it can be bent around curves.
However, we now know that lead causes serious health problems and have banned the use of lead pipe in plumbing.

Some older homes still have lead pipe for supply lines; in some areas, lead was used until the 1980s.

A water pipe that bends is probably lead. To test, cut into it slightly with a knife; lead is much softer than steel, and a knife will make a gouge with moderate pressure.

Remove any lead supply lines and replace them with copper pipe.

If your main supply line is lead, the danger is probably minimal, and it would be costly to have it replaced. To be safe, run water for several minutes in the morning before drinking. Many municipalities with lead pipes now add a trace amount of phosphate to the water supply, which causes a lining to form on the inside of the pipes and virtually eliminates leaching of lead into the water. (Over time, mineral-laden water has the same effect.)

Copper pipe joined with solder that contains lead is not usually a problem, since such a small amount of lead is involved. Have your water tested for lead content if you have concerns.

PIPE OPTIONS

¾" black steel

1" black steel

Cast iron

4" PVC

3" PVC

2" PVC

¾" PVC

½" galvanized steel

½" rigid copper

¾" rigid copper

¾" galvanized steel

½" flexible copper

¼" flexible copper

BLACK STEEL is found in the pipe section of your supply outlet, but don't use it for water. It's for gas only.

CAST IRON was the material of choice for soil stacks until the 1960s. It is very strong and durable, but extremely heavy and difficult to install. Anchor it securely to the house's framing and seal joints with oakum and molten lead (a job for the pros) or with no-hub rubber fittings. Cast iron is difficult to cut and place. Use plastic instead; transition fittings make it easy to join plastic to cast iron.

PVC PLASTIC is the most common choice for drain lines both inside the house and underground. It comes in 10- and 20-foot lengths, is easy to work with and will last nearly forever. Cut it with most any kind of saw and join it with glue. PVC is sometimes used for supply lines, but many localities forbid it because the joints can fail after years of holding supply-line pressures. Schedule 40 PVC is the most common choice for residential work. Schedule 80, which is thicker, is used in commercial applications and when threaded nipples are required. Class 125 PVC has very thin walls and is permitted only for irrigation systems. CPVC, often gray in color, withstands higher temperatures than PVC. Black ABS plastic was once common for drain lines but is out of favor.

GALVANIZED STEEL is the strongest material for supply lines (and is also used for branch drains), but it can clog with rust and mineral deposits, and that reduces water pressure. Rusty joints are prone to leak. Galvanized steel requires special machinery for cutting and threading, but you can sidestep that problem by buying it precut and threaded. Just be sure to measure precisely. When possible, make the transition from steel to copper when installing a new line. Also, use a dielectric union, which keeps molecules of dissimilar metals from justifying from one to the other and clogging the joint.

COPPER PIPE, rigid or flexible, is most commonly used for supply lines but is also used for drains. Rigid pipe comes in 20- and 10-foot lengths. Type M copper pipe is strong enough for most residential work; types L and K are thicker and may be required for main supply lines. Flexible copper comes in 60-foot and 100-foot coils. It is most commonly used to supply water to such appliances as an ice maker and dishwasher. Once you get the hang of cutting and assembling copper, you'll be a pro in no time. It cuts easily with a tubing cutter. Better rigid and flexible pipe can be soldered, but the flexible stuff is often connected with compression fittings.

FITTINGS

45° copper elbow

Brass drop ell

90° copper elbow

Galvanized steel elbow

Galvanized steel reducer

W alk down the plumbing aisle in a home center, and you may find yourself bewildered by the variety of available fittings. Relax—choosing the right fitting is not as complicated as it looks. Most fittings have obvious functions, and once you plan your project, finding the fittings is easy.

Supply fittings are identified by their material, function, and size. They guide your water supply through the twists and turns that lead to your fixtures.

SUPPLY FITTINGS

Supply fittings come in five types: elbows, tees, caps, couplings, and unions. Buy extra elbows and tees; they're cheap, and it's easy to overlook a turn or two. Besides, a few leftover pieces are preferable to making extra trips to the hardware store. Here's what these supply fittings do:

Copper 45° elbow

Copper tee

Copper coupling

Copper fitting reducer

Copper cap

Copper male adapter

Copper adapter slip

Galvanized 90° elbow

Galvanized nipple

Galvanized cap

Galvanized reducer tee

Galvanized reducer

Galvanized coupling

Galvanized union

Galvanized 90° elbow

Plastic bushing

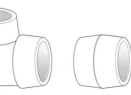

Plastic tee

Plastic coupling

ELBOWS: Elbows (also referred to as ells) change direction and are available in 45- and 90-degree angles.

■ **STANDARD ELLS** have two female openings the same size.

■ **REDUCING ELLS** have one opening smaller than the other.

■ **STREET ELLS** have one female end and one male end; they're handy for tight turns.

■ **DROP ELLS** help when you are making a turn into a fixture. They have flanges with holes so you can attach them securely.

TEES: These T-shape fittings divert water to another line and have three female openings at right angles to one another.

■ **STRAIGHT TEES** have three openings all the same size.

■ **REDUCING TEES** have one opening smaller than the other two. In the most common reducing tee, the run-through openings are the same size, and the branch opening is smaller.

CAPS AND COUPLINGS: Use a cap when you want a pipe to end. Have some handy so if you need to leave a job partially finished, you can cap it off and restore water pressure. Use a coupling to join sections of pipe. Standard couplings have female openings at either end; a reducing coupling allows you to change pipe size. With an adapter coupling you can change from glued or soldered joints to a threaded joint. Use a transition coupling to change from steel to plastic or from copper to plastic.

UNIONS: Whenever you are using threaded steel pipe, you will need at least one union; you cannot screw pipe into both ends at once. A union allows you to couple and uncouple sections without turning either section.

Use a dielectric union (*see page 24*) to change from steel to copper. It blocks the tiny current that occurs when the two metals touch. Without the dielectric union, this current would transfer particles of copper to the steel pipe and corrode and plug the joint.

DWV FITTINGS

The liquid that drain, waste, and vent pipes carry away is not under pressure, so it can't be impeded by any sharp angles and bends. DWV fittings change direction gradually, and there are more types of them than supply fittings to allow for the slope needed for drains and waste pipes and the special situations that need to be plumbed around. If the common types of fittings shown here do not solve your problem, a plumbing-supplies dealer should be able to point you toward the right fitting.

BENDS AND ELBOWS: Fittings used to change flow direction are called bends and elbows (ells).

■ **QUARTER BEND:** An ell that makes a 90-degree turn is called a quarter bend because it turns one quarter of a circle. Quarter bends can have a short, medium, or long radius. Medium- and long-turn quarter bends are called sweeps.

■ **ODD ANGLES:** A 45-degree ell is called an eighth bend, and a 22½-degree ell is a sixteenth bend. Fifth and sixth bends make 72-degree and 60-degree turns, respectively. In tight situations, these angles come in handy.

■ **OTHER BENDS:** A closet bend is designed for a toilet. An offset bend allows you to move the pipe over a bit.

When space is tight, a street ell may be the solution. Its one male end can be fit directly into another fitting.

TEES AND WYES: These fittings form a T or Y shape to accommodate a branch line. Each opening may be a different size. The two openings in a tee or wye that line up so you can see through them both are the *run* openings. The opening that projects at an angle from the run is called the branch. When ordering a tee or wye, specify run sizes first, then branch size. For example, to get a 3-inch-diameter wye with a 2-inch-diameter branch, request a "3 by 3 by 2 wye."

CROSSES AND DOUBLE-WYES: These fittings have two branches coming into the run. No more than two sizes are ever involved. A 3 by 2 double wye has a run of 3 inches and two 2-inch branches at opposite sides of the run.

ADAPTERS AND TRANSITION PIECES: A wide variety of fittings allow you to join different materials and different sizes. Adapting and reducing couplings can join any combination of plastic, copper, and cast-iron DWV pipe. They can even be used for galvanized steel pipe from which the threads

have been cut. These transition couplings have an inner section that compensates for the different pipe dimensions and their outside dimensions are made to match the size pipe they're joining. They can be a bit expensive but will save you plenty of work.

Use a trap adapter to make the transition from pipe to tubular trap materials (*see page 16*).

CLEANOUTS: At convenient locations, install a wye with a cleanout insert instead of a coupling. The more cleanouts you have, the easier it will be for you to auger the line if it ever becomes clogged.

A long-turn 90-degree bend (above) and a regular-radius sanitary tee (left) exhibit the gradual bends needed in drainpipes and waste pipes.

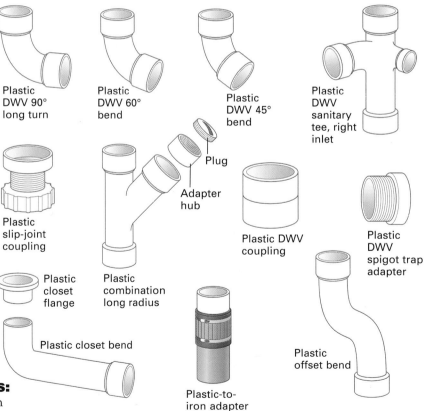

Plastic DWV 90° long turn

Plastic DWV 60° bend

Plastic DWV 45° bend

Plastic DWV sanitary tee, right inlet

Plastic slip-joint coupling

Plug

Adapter hub

Plastic DWV coupling

Plastic DWV spigot trap adapter

Plastic closet flange

Plastic combination long radius

Plastic closet bend

Plastic-to-iron adapter

Plastic offset bend

Drainpipes and waste pipes are designed with bends that are more gradual than those on supply pipes. They also come in more varied shapes to cope with sloped runs across walls and between joists.

Solder

Propane torch

Spark lighter

Flux

Flux brush

Wire fitting brush

Tubing cutter

Even a veteran do-it-yourselfer will joke about a plumbing job taking at least four trips to the hardware store. In addition to having the essential tools shown here, have plenty of spare fittings (especially elbows and tees) on hand. That way, you can spend more time doing the job and less time chasing around for missing pieces.

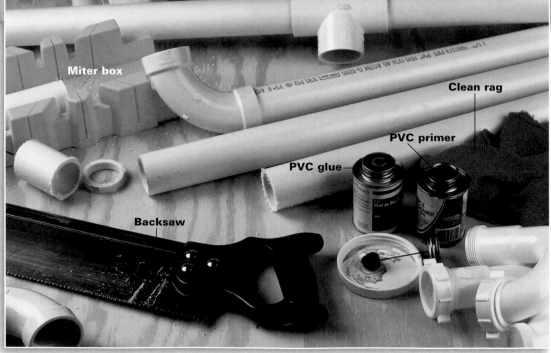

Miter box

Clean rag

PVC primer

PVC glue

Backsaw

SKILLS & TOOLS

Some construction skills, such as building cabinets or laying a brick wall, take years to perfect. Not plumbing. Though you may never work as fast as a plumber, after only a few hours of practice, you will be able to make pipe joints like a pro. This chapter shows you how to work copper, plastic, cast iron, and steel.

One tip that's as solid as steel pipe: Buy good tools. Better tools will save you time.

Start with a tape measure and a felt-tip pen for marking all types of pipe. Also, buy plumber's paper or sanding screen for cleaning the ends of copper pipes and for removing burrs from plastic pipes.

Each type of material calls for its own array of tools. We've listed them below and shown them in the photographs. Special tools needed for working with copper: a **propane torch** with a **spark lighter** (go ahead—spend extra for the self-igniting model), a **wire brush** to clean the inside of pipes, a **flux brush**, and a **tubing cutter**. Supplies include **flux** and **solder.**

To cut and glue plastic pipe, the only special tools you need are a **backsaw** and **miter box** for cutting

pipe evenly or, for small dimensions, a tubing cutter. For joining pipes, have a clean **rag,** along with cans of **primer** and **PVC glue.**

To install galvanized steel and black pipe, have two **pipe wrenches** and a **hacksaw** or reciprocating saw with a metal-cutting blade. To loosen very tight pipes, get a **"cheater" pipe**—a 2-foot length of 1¼-inch pipe that you slide onto the handle of a pipe wrench to increase your leverage.

A pair of **tongue-and-groove pliers** will see plenty of plumbing service. And you'll need **Teflon tape** or **pipe joint compound** for joining pipes and fittings.

Cheater pipe

Hacksaw

Teflon tape

Pipe wrench

Tongue-and-groove pliers

FIXTURE TRAPS

Fixing a leaky trap ranks among the most common household repairs. Though the function of traps is easy to understand, working on them can be surprisingly difficult—the human body is simply not designed for such a tight squeeze. But even before you have a go at disassembly, decide what material you'll use for replacement. If it's just a leak you're fixing, the problem may be only the gaskets—they often dry out and crack.

TYPES

Traps are made of thin-wall brass (plated or unplated) or plastic. Chrome-plated traps can corrode and need to be replaced after eight to 10 years. Plastic lasts longer, but if the trap will be visible, you may want to spend extra for shiny brass. Use thicker 17-gauge rather than the standard 20-gauge. A bathroom trap is 1¼ inches in diameter; a kitchen trap is 1½ inches.

A P-trap looks somewhat like a P laid on its side. It exits out the wall. Less common (and prohibited in some areas), S-traps take an extra turn so they can exit into the floor.

TAKING TRAPS APART

Traps come apart fairly easily. Here's a description of the pieces—starting at the drain or strainer and working down.

TAILPIECE: A straight tube threaded or snugged with a nut to the strainer. A tailpiece can be threaded to an extension or unthreaded to slip into the trap.

EXTENSION: Unthreaded at the bottom to slip into the trap.

SLIP NUT: Allows an unthreaded piece to be inserted into a threaded one so its length can be adjusted to fit. A slip nut compresses a neoprene washer to seal the joint.

TRAP PIECE: J-or 8-shaped, usually threaded on both ends for slip nuts.

TRAP ARM: An unthreaded straight or curved piece between the trap and the branch drain line or waste pipe.

Once you have the pieces removed—and depending on the problem that caused you to take them apart in the first place—you can auger the line (*see page 28*), and clean the trap or replace it.

INSTALLATION

Assemble all the pieces before you start tightening nuts. Loosely attach the assembly at both ends and adjust the slip joints so everything fits without binding. Then give the trap a rigorous test: Plug the drain, fill the sink with hot water, and pull the plug. Lay clean newspapers beneath the trap and watch carefully for leaks. Straighten the tubing and retighten the nuts as necessary. Trap joints are not very strong, so they can become dislodged if they get bumped.

Waste pipe
Sink basin
Tailpiece
Neoprene washer
Extension
Slip nuts
Trap arm
J-bend

A P-trap uses a surprising number of parts. Put the slip nuts on unthreaded pieces first, then the washers. Then insert the pipes into the pieces with threads.

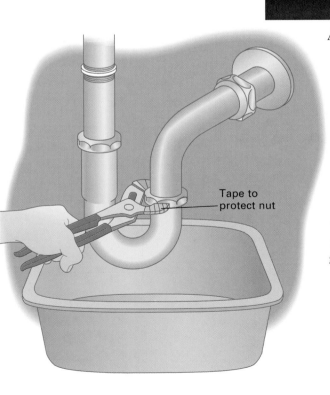

Tape to protect nut

When assembling a trap, make sure the pieces join in a straight line. If you force a crooked joint, it will likely leak.

COMPRESSION FITTINGS AND COPPER TUBING

Compression fittings, used with flexible copper tubing, are designed for connections that may need to be taken apart someday. They form a seal when a compression nut is tightened against a ferrule. Shutoff valves use compression fittings; dishwashers, ice makers, and hot-water dispensers also use them. Most building codes do not allow them inside walls.

KINKS: Working with copper tubing won't require special skills, but you must be careful. The tubing will kink if you bend it too sharply (something that is distressingly easy to do). A kink limits water flow severely and may break and leak. It cannot be fixed; you'll have to start again with a new piece. Remove the tubing carefully from its box, uncoiling it in long, sweeping bends. For turns, use a tubing bender.

CUTTING: Cut the tubing with a tubing cutter (*see page 18*). Don't use a hacksaw; sawing will bend the tubing out of round. If the tubing isn't perfectly round, the nut and ferrule will be difficult to attach and may leak.

ASSEMBLY: Slide the nut onto the tube, and slip on the ferrule. Fit the tube straight into the fitting, pushing it as far as it will go. Slide the nut down onto the fitting (the ferrule will slide with it) and tighten.

Take special care when tightening the fittings. Not only is tubing easily bent, but compression fittings are often connected to valves that are not sturdy. In most cases, it is best to use two wrenches or pliers, and don't overtighten.

A compression union, with threads on each end, uses two nuts and two ferrules to join lengths of flexible tubing. Like all compression fittings, it forms a seal by tightening the copper ferrule to the tubing. No pipe joint compound is needed.

An inexpensive, springlike tubing bender will help you avoid kinks.

Kink

Slip the tubing in the bender and apply pressure by hand.

Tubing bender

Ferrule

Compression union

Compression nut

Use two wrenches to attach a union (left) to copper pipe or to attach a supply line to a shutoff valve (below).

FLARE FITTINGS

If you pull apart a fitting in copper line and find that the ends of the tubes have been expanded into a flared shape, you have an old-fashioned flare fitting. Making a fitting like this calls for a flaring tool as well as special fittings.

Flare fittings are not difficult to make, but it is not worth your while to buy the tool and materials. Just cut the tubing ends off with a tubing cutter (or cut replacement tubing) and install a compression fitting.

Stabilize fitting with an adjustable wrench

SWEATING COPPER JOINTS

Copper pipe is the material of choice for most new supply-line installations. It may sound like a lot of trouble to cut the pieces and solder (or "sweat") them together, but with a little practice, you'll be sweating joints routinely.

PREPARATION

Handle copper pipe carefully. Dented ends are difficult to join. Use a tape measure to determine the pipe span and remember to include the depth of the fittings (*see page 10*). Mark the cut line with a felt-tip pen.

CUTTING: A tubing cutter makes a cleaner and straighter cut than a hacksaw and severs the pipe without denting the end. Slip the pipe into the cutter, and screw the cutting wheel tight at the cutoff mark. Rotate the cutter all the way around, tighten the knob further, rotate in the opposite direction, and repeat until the cutting wheel cuts through. Do not apply too much pressure or you will dent the pipe. Use the reamer blade on the tubing cutter to remove the lip on the inside of the pipe.

Dry-fit the pieces to make sure of your measurements before you solder them. As you gain experience, you may want to cut four or five pieces, dry-fit them, clean and flux them, reassemble, and solder all the pieces at once.

CLEANING: Copper oxidizes when exposed to air, and the oxides coat the pipe with a

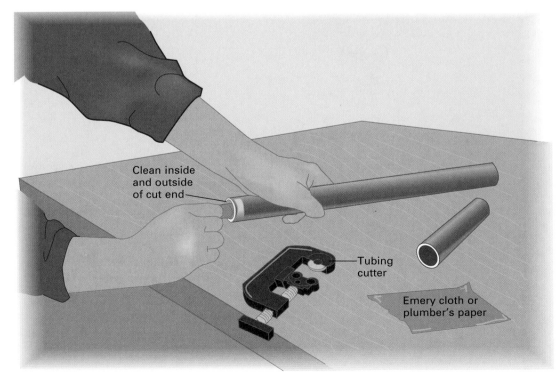

Tubing cutter

thin layer. This coating must be completely removed whenever you make a joint—solder won't stick to oxides.

Don't underestimate this step: The strength of the joint depends for the most part on how thoroughly the copper pipe has been cleaned. You can use sandpaper and steel wool to clean copper, but emery cloth or a sanding screen does the job best.

Hold the emery cloth around the end of the pipe with one hand, and twist the pipe with the other hand until the pipe end is gleaming. Then twist a wire fitting brush (*see page 14*), or a piece of emery cloth wrapped around your finger, inside the fitting until the interior looks as shiny as the pipe end. About five twists should do the job.

APPLYING FLUX: Flux is an acidic paste that chemically cleans copper. Solder will adhere only to surfaces that have been fluxed. Use a flux brush to scoop up a moderate amount of flux and paint the end of the pipe to the depth the fitting will cover. Also paint

Even if the copper pipe or fitting looks clean and shiny, polish it inside and out with emery cloth, steel wool, or sandpaper to remove oxides and to assure a strong joint.

Clean inside and outside of cut end

Tubing cutter

Emery cloth or plumber's paper

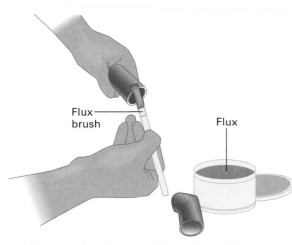

After cleaning the end of the pipe with a sanding screen or emery cloth, brush on flux.

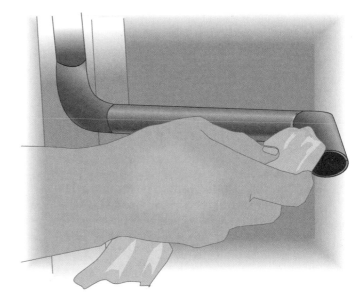

When sweating copper, always protect combustible materials from the heat of the torch. A heavy-duty cookie sheet makes a handy shield.

the inside of the fitting, using a circular swipe that carries completely around the inside of the pipe. Insert the pipe into the fitting and twist it a half turn or so, to smear the flux evenly and to cover any spots you may have missed. Wipe off excess flux that squeezes out of the fitting.

SOLDER THE JOINTS

Before you fire up your torch, support the pipes securely in place and make sure that beams, joists, and wiring won't be burned by the flame. Protect such surfaces with flame-resistant materials.

Uncoil about a foot of solder and bend the end into a shape that will make it easy to apply it to the joint. Light the torch with a striker, and adjust the flame so that the inner blue cone is about 2 inches long.

Use the tip of the blue cone to heat the fitting. Do not heat the pipe. Keep the flame on the side of the fitting from where you'll touch the solder, but move the flame slowly back and forth to avoid frying the flux.

When the flux starts to sizzle, and smoke appears, touch the solder to the edge of the fitting and see if it melts. If it does, move the flame away from the joint (don't burn anything else) and keep the solder in contact

with the edge. It will run completely around the joint and be drawn into it.

When one drop overflows, withdraw the solder. Turn off the torch and immediately wipe the joint with a damp rag. If the solder beads up and will not flow into the joint, either the joint is not clean or it has too little flux. Take it apart and start again, or the joint may fail eventually.

When the joints are sweated, support the pipe where possible with copper pipe supports at 3-foot intervals. They will help keep the pipes from shuddering when the water is turned on and off.

Wipe away excess solder right away. Take care not to bump the joint while the solder is still hot. If there is a residue of flux, wipe it away after a minute or so.

SWEATING BRASS VALVES

Sweat pipes into a brass valve as you would into a fitting. However, if the valve has some plastic parts inside, disassemble the valve to avoid melting them. Reassemble only after the joints have cooled.

GLUING PLASTIC PIPE

Putting together plastic pipe might seem as easy as assembling a child's toy, but it does have its challenges. It is easier to cut and assemble than its rival materials, but once a joint is made, it cannot be taken apart nor can it be turned or adjusted. That means you'll have to use alignment marks and dry-fit carefully before making the final joints.

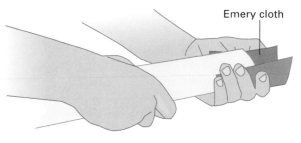

1. *To join plastic pipe, first use sandpaper or emery cloth to remove burrs inside and outside of the cut end.*

Emery cloth

MEASURING AND CUTTING

Before making any cuts, visualize the arrangement and orientation of the fittings and pipes. Lay them out and temporarily install them if you can. When you measure, be sure to include the distance that the pipe must extend into the socket of the fitting.

MEASURING: Here's a handy technique to measure a long length of pipe:
■ Straddle the pipe. It may help to rest it between your knees.
■ Grasp the pipe with one hand, resting your thumb on the spot where you estimate that you'll cut.
■ Hook the end of the tape measure over the far end of the pipe and pull it toward you.
■ With the thumb of your free hand, mark the exact location of the cut. Holding your thumb on the spot, retract the tape measure.
■ Slide a pipe cutter to your thumb and tighten it, or mark the cut mark with a saw.

CUTTING: A variety of cutting tools will work: a fine-toothed backsaw and a miter box, a power miter box, or a tubing cutter. If you are cutting small-diameter plastic supply pipe, a handheld PVC cutter will do the job with a minimum of trouble. After cutting, remove burrs inside the pipe with emery cloth or a

Backsaw

Miter box

knife. Hold the pipe so the burrs fall out, not in. Then wipe a rag or the thumb of a gloved hand around the inside of the fitting.

DRY-FITTING AND ALIGNING: Push the pipe about halfway into the fitting. (Don't push so hard that it's difficult to pull out.) If possible, make a dry run of four or five pipes or fittings as they will lay out in your installation.

You'll need to align pipes and fittings precisely; otherwise, they'll aim the next pieces off in the wrong direction. Once your pieces are dry-fitted correctly, make alignment marks on both the fittings and the pipes so that you can put them back together in exactly the same way later. A felt-tipped pen works well for this, but the mark can be inadvertently wiped away. For that reason, some plumbers scratch lines with a nail.

JOINING WITH GLUE

From here on, readiness is everything. Once the glue is applied, you have only a few seconds to work. If there is an obstacle you forgot to remove, if you can't find the alignment lines, or if you don't know exactly how you will assemble in an awkward location, you may end up blowing the joint, which will mean starting all over. So get your ducks in a row before you begin.

PRIMER: Coat the outside ends of pipes and the inside sockets of fittings with primer, using the ball-shaped applicator. Primer removes the glaze, cleans off wax and dirt, and will ensure a strong seal. It will take the primer less than a minute to dry. Always screw the cap back on immediately; it dries quickly and spills easily.

CEMENT: When you open the cement can, you'll find the applicator will have more glue than you need for one swipe. Skim off some

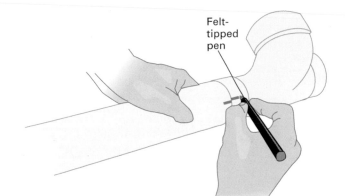

Felt-
tipped
pen

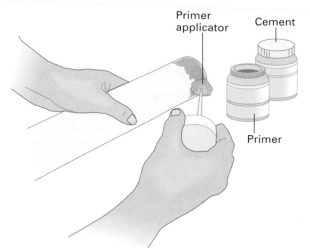

Primer
applicator

Cement

Primer

2. *Once the glue has set, you cannot twist the pipe even slightly to correct the alignment. Dry-fit the pipe and fitting first, and mark the alignment with a felt-tipped pen.*

3. *To assure a sealed joint, prime the pipe. The color lets you (and your inspector) see that no spots are missed. Prime the inside of the fitting as well.*

on the lip of the opening and apply cement to the inside of the fitting and the outside of the pipe—just to the depth it will slip into the fitting.

Back off your alignment marks about a quarter turn. Then push the pipe into the socket, twisting it to make sure the cement is smeared evenly and the alignment marks match up. Immediately wipe off the excess cement that wells out of the new joint. (If no cement comes out, you have not applied enough.)

CURING: Hold the pipe in place for 15–30 seconds, until the cement locks the pipe in the fitting. During the next two minutes, it will be just barely possible to remove the pipe.

How long do you have to wait before you use the pipe? Plastic DWV pipe usually is ready to carry unpressurized water within 15 minutes of installation. For supply lines where the water will be under pressure, you will have to wait longer. Read the can for curing times.

PIPE SUPPORT: Continue to assemble the remaining pieces in the same way. Support horizontal runs every 3–4 feet with galvanized plumber's tape (wrap the pipe with duct tape first) or plastic pipe supports, which snap to the pipe and attach to framing with plastic rods.

Cement applicator

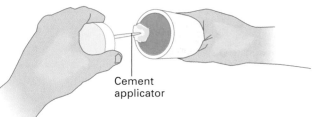

Alignment marks

4. *Apply pipe cement to the outside of the pipe and the inside of the fitting; push the fitting onto the pipe so that, by giving it about a quarter turn, your marks will align. Wipe away excess.*

CAST IRON

Cast iron was once the workhorse of house DWV systems, but it is so expensive and difficult to work with that virtually no current residential construction codes require it.

Old cast-iron pipes were joined together with a hub-and-spigot arrangement. The hub was the female side of the joint. The male spigot end was inserted into the hub, the joint was packed with a fiber called oakum, then it was sealed with molten lead. To do the job, plumbers needed small furnaces to melt the lead, caulking irons to pack the oakum, and a ladle for pouring the lead into joints. Today professionals occasionally still install cast iron, but wherever possible they use rubber no-hub connectors instead of lead and oakum.

No-hub joints replace the hub-and-spigot joints and make working with cast iron less difficult. Still, the pipe itself is extremely heavy. Anytime you are working with it, make sure it is firmly supported.

CUTTING

It is no easy matter to cut cast iron, especially when the pipe is situated in a tight or hard-to-reach spot.

If you can get to the pipe, the quickest way to cut cast iron is with a circular saw that is equipped with a metal-cutting blade. Wear safety glasses: Sparks and small particles will fly dramatically. If the pipe is in a wall or a floor, cutting it with a circular saw won't work. Use a reciprocating saw with a metal-cutting blade. Cast iron is hard; cutting it will be slow going. If these tools won't work, rent a soil-pipe cutter (*below*).

RENT A SOIL-PIPE CUTTER

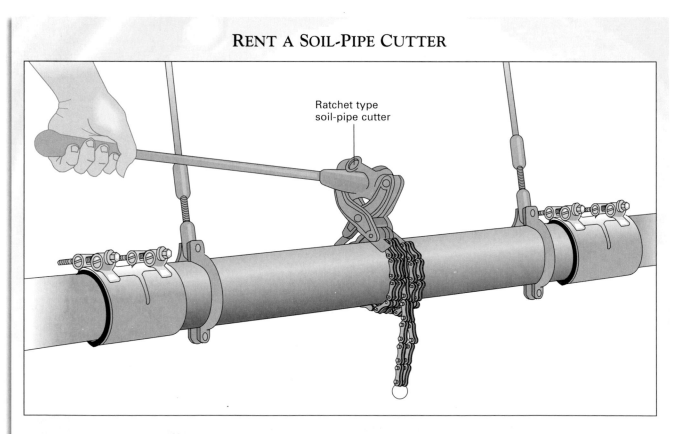

Ratchet type soil-pipe cutter

Other than a circular saw that's fitted with a metal-cutting blade, a rented soil-pipe cutter, or snap cutter, is the easiest way to cut cast iron. (Choose the ratchet-type of soil-pipe cutter *shown above* instead of the scissors-type.) A soil-pipe cutter has a chain of cutting wheels and a lever that tightens the cutting chain around the pipe. The tightened wheels incise a dotted line around the pipe. Once the cutting wheels of the soil-pipe cutter have dug in deeply enough, the pipe fractures. Because cast iron is brittle, the break is usually clean.

When using a soil-pipe cutter, make room for the chain if possible by supporting both sides of the cut with 2×4s. When you wrap the pipe with the chain, make sure that it forms a circle around the pipe, and not a spiral.

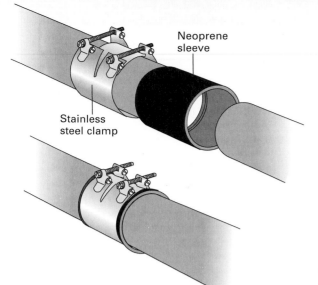

Neoprene sleeve

Stainless steel clamp

Today, cast iron is joined with a neoprene sleeve and a stainless steel clamp instead of a lead-sealed hub and spigot. This coupling is ideal for joining plastic pipe to cast iron.

FLEXIBLE COUPLING

Cast iron can be joined to other cast iron or to plastic pipe with a no-hub coupling, which is made of two pieces: a neoprene sleeve and a stainless-steel clamp. A variety of couplings are available, so you can connect almost any size plastic pipe to any size cast-iron pipe. Here's how.

Slide the clamp down the cast-iron pipe; it will be loose. Slip the sleeve onto the pipe to its center, making sure it is uniformly tight all the way around, with no folds or creases. Then insert the plastic pipe into the other half of the neoprene sleeve. This may be difficult because the fit is so tight, and it might help to roll the sleeve back before inserting the pipe. Make sure both pipes are pushed all the way to the center of the sleeve.

Once the sleeve is tight on both pipes, slip the clamp over it (you may have to loosen it some). Tighten the screws evenly, shifting back and forth between them as you work.

TYING IN WITH A SADDLE TEE

If you add a new drain line to a cast-iron soil stack, one option is to cut a section out of the stack and then install a plastic tee fitting using no-hub couplings. However, you'll have to check that once the cut is made, both ends of the cast-iron pipe are strongly supported. This can be difficult; often there are hundreds of pounds of pipe above and below the cut.

A saddle tee makes the job much easier, but check local codes to make sure it is acceptable in your area. Purchase a saddle

To break into a cast-iron soil pipe, use a circular saw with a metal-cutting blade. For a saddle-tee fitting, plunge-cut a square. Take care to keep the cutout from falling into the pipe.

tee with dimension matching the old and new lines. Cut a hole in the cast-iron pipe at the spot where you want the new drain line to enter. See the instructions on the saddle tee's package for the correct size of hole. It can be square, and it does not have to be precise, but it must not be too large.

Metal-cutting blade

Use a circular saw with a metal-cutting blade to cut the hole. (Wear safety glasses.) Rest the saw's base plate firmly on the pipe, and retract the blade guard to make a "plunge" cut. Start the motor and lower the blade slowly, holding the saw firmly so it cannot skip away. Cut carefully so none of the cut lines will be left uncovered by the saddle tee. To make sure the cutout piece does not fall into the pipe, avoid completely cutting one corner. Pry the cutout section away with a screwdriver.

Use a knife to cut a hole in the neoprene that is slightly larger than the hole in the pipe. Put the neoprene in place, then press the fitting over it. Slide the U-shaped clamps from the back of the pipe, attach the nuts, and tighten. Test the fitting by draining water from a sink above the tee. If the saddle tee leaks, tighten the clamps.

Neoprene

Saddle tee

A saddle tee is the easiest way to add a drain line to a cast-iron system. Sealed with a piece of neoprene, it clamps over a hole cut in the pipe with a circular saw.

STEEL PIPE

G alvanized steel resists denting better than copper, but that's about its only advantage. Installing it is hard work, and it is not nearly as long-lasting as copper. So if you're working with a water line, make the transition to copper whenever possible.

Do not use copper for gas lines: A chemical reaction causes the copper to flake, sending harmful particles into the valves and burners of gas appliances.

Use a reciprocating saw with a metal-cutting blade to cut steel pipe. Be sure the pipe doesn't vibrate filling joints loose and create new leaks.

Make a rough drawing showing where all of your pipes will go, measuring for each length, and account for the socket depth of the fittings. Use elbows to make turns and use tees to split one line into two.

Professionals who install steel pipe regularly have large, expensive machinery that cuts and threads the pipe at the job site. The homeowner's solution is to purchase ready-cut lengths of pipe from a home center or plumbing-supply center. (Call around for prices; they can vary widely.)

Do-it-yourselfers who install steel pipe are often surprised at how much time they spend running to the plumbing-supply source. Not only are there all those fittings to keep track of, but it is nearly impossible at the beginning of a job to determine exactly which lengths of pipe you will need. One way to cut down on shopping trips is to buy a collection of nipples—lengths of pipe 6 inches long or shorter. You can even buy a box of nipples containing all the sizes, in ½-inch increments. The nipples will increase your options so that you can finish a run at the right point.

MIXED MEDIA

Braided supply

Stop valve

Copper

Dielectric union

Steel pipe

Union   Nipple   Tee

90° elbow

Even a straightforward extension of a galvanized-steel supply line can involve several different fittings and types of pipe. This example shows a supply extension (either hot or cold water) with a new stop valve and braided-metal supply attaching to a fixture. The steel pipe is extended through a dielectric union (*see page 12*) to a run of copper supply pipe for an upstairs fixture.

When adding or replacing plumbing, make the job as easy as possible by assembling sections in advance. In this example, all of the galvanized steel could be assembled on a workbench. Such prefabrication not only is easier to do, it results in better joints. However, prefabrication does require careful measuring and a knack for visualizing the completed installation. If the completed assembly doesn't quite fit, remove it and make adjustments by changing the lengths of the nipples.

BREAKING INTO A LINE

Pipe threads go only one way, so they have to be assembled (and disassembled) in order; you cannot simply remove a pipe in the middle of a run and install a new one. You will need to find or install a union. This is a special fitting that can accept pipes from both directions at once and attaches (or loosens) them without requiring that they be turned.

Shut off the gas or water before dismantling or cutting steel pipes. If a union already exists nearby, examine it closely to see which direction the ring nut is facing. Put one wrench on the union nut and turn the ring nut counterclockwise with another wrench.

If there is no existing union, cut a pipe with a hacksaw or a reciprocating saw equipped with a metal-cutting blade. Then you can unscrew both sides of the cut pipe. You will need to install a union when you do the new plumbing.

Once you've cut into and removed a section, a union lets you add new pipe or tee to a line without rebuilding most of the run.

JOINING STEEL

Before you start screwing steel pipe joints together, wrap pipe threads with Teflon tape or apply pipe joint compound to the threads. Wrap two or three windings in a clockwise direction; if you go counterclockwise, the tape may peel off.

Starting at one end of the installation, assemble the pipes in order, tightening each one as you go. Tighten first with tongue-and-groove pliers, then use a pipe wrench. Keep tightening until you have to bear down hard with the wrench.

To install a union, first slip the ring nut on the shoulder piece. Apply Teflon tape or joint compound to the pipe end threads and tighten the shoulder piece and male-threaded nut to the pipes. Then apply tape or joint compound to the threads of the male-threaded nut (but not its face) and tighten the ring nut to it.

Use a second pipe wrench to stabilize the pipe or fitting while tightening a joint.

Gas line

Drip leg

Slope a long run of gas line and add a drip leg near the end to prevent buildup of moisture.

GAS LINES

Note: Gas is dangerous. Unless you have experience installing steel pipe, hire a pro to work on gas lines. Slight gas leaks that are not immediately apparent can have dire consequences.

Turn off the gas at the meter or the appliance line before beginning any work. Keep the area ventilated because some gas will be left in the lines.

Be sure you use the right size pipe. For most residential work, ¾-inch pipe will be large enough. Use ½-inch pipe only for short runs. A gas pipe that is too small will cause an appliance to malfunction.

A small amount of moisture collects in gas lines. For this reason, slope long horizontal runs and install a drip leg near the end to collect water.

After installing the pipe, connect it to the appliance with a flexible gas line. It will have flared compression fittings at each end.

Turn on the gas and make a thorough inspection for leaks: Test every new joint by using a plant sprayer to coat it (all sides) with a soap-and-water solution, then look for bubbles. Check all the joints and the fittings, which occasionally have pinholes.

If augering your drain lines does not make them drain fast enough, or if drains on the bottom floor back up, your sewer line may need to be augered. Rent a power auger and run it through a cleanout in your sewer line, or hire someone who specializes in rodding.

MAINTAINING PIPES

Sluggish or stopped-up drains are seldom the result of faulty pipes. Clogs almost always result from the gunk buildup.

Prevent clogs by keeping solid matter out. Keep the strainers in place on your sinks and bathtubs. Wads of hair cause some of the most tenacious blockages; regularly cleaning hair out of your tub or shower drain is well worth the effort. If you don't have a grease trap or catch basin (see page 8), grease can plug your main line. Pour your kitchen grease into cans and dispose of it with the garbage.

Remember that the toilet is the only plumbing fixture in your house designed to handle solid waste. Many plumbers even recommend that you limit your use of the garbage disposer: It grinds food into a paste, some of which can collect in drainpipes.

This chapter will show you the basic ways to reach and remove these clogs. If a drain is stopped up, start with the simplest techniques: Clean and remove a strainer, and use a plunger (see page 28) or pressure from an aerosol remover or garden hose. If that doesn't work, move on to augering and, if necessary, dismantling pipes.

Familiarize yourself with all the points of entry in your drainage system. Some sink traps have small cleanout nuts; simply unscrew one to clear the way for an auger. There should be several cleanouts on large drainpipes allowing you to auger them without taking them apart.

UNCLOGGING TECHNIQUES

Soap scum, hair, and small objects dropped down the drain (only by the kids, of course) will collect wherever a pipe makes a sharp bend. Traps are the first step. They not only prevent gases from entering your house (*see page 8*), they also keep obstructions from lodging farther down the line. In a well-designed system, the trap will be the sharpest turn your drain makes, so they're the first place to look if you have a clog.

FOR OPENERS

Before you start dismantling pipes, give the easiest techniques a try.

CLEAN UNDER THE STOPPER: Often the underside of a sink stopper will accumulate hair and scum. Pull the stopper up, and remove it, if possible. Don't force it; some stoppers unlock with a twist; others are attached to a rod that you have to detach below the sink. Remove any debris.

PLUNGING: Before plunging a sink, stop up any overflow outlets with wet rags. On a double-bowl sink, have a helper block the other opening by holding the stopper firmly in place.

Make sure the plunger cup forms a tight seal around the opening; coating it with petroleum jelly is a favorite plumber's trick. Work the plunger rapidly up and down, both pushing and pulling the blockage to loosen it. Do not use a plunger if you've already used

Flanged cup

drain cleaner; the caustic liquid may spatter.

To remove obstructions in a toilet, seat the plunger in the toilet so it seals the opening; you should feel the suction. Push and pull vigorously a dozen times or more. To test the toilet, pour in a couple gallons of water rather than risking an overflow with flushing.

CLEAN THE TRAP: If your sink trap has a cleanout nut (most do not), unscrew it and let the water drain out. Otherwise, unscrew the slip nuts and remove the trap piece (*see page 16*). Clean the trap out; if it is full of gunk, you may have solved the problem. If the trap is clean, you'll probably need to auger.

DRAIN CLEANER: Use drain cleaner only for a sluggish drain, never on a drain that is completely stopped up; it can make the clog worse, and some cleaners may damage pipes or gaskets (no matter what the label says). In addition, if the cleaner doesn't work, you'll have a caustic mess on your hands if you have to dismantle the trap. When you're using a drain cleaner, wear heavy clothing that you are willing to discard, and pour carefully so you don't get splashed. Don't plunge or disassemble a drain with cleaner in it.

AUGERING

A plumbing auger, often called a snake, is a long flexible cable made of coiled steel. An inexpensive model with a handheld crank will clear many clogs. If you have much augering to do, or if a hand-operated model won't reach, consider buying a handheld power auger, which looks like a drill. For cleaning main drains, you need a power auger that stands on the floor (*see page 26*).

Do not attempt heavy-duty augering unless your auger cable has a cable running through its center. The center cable keeps the auger from kinking, and if the coiled cable breaks, it will allow you to retrieve it.

AUGERING A SINK: In most cases, you won't be able to push the auger down the sink drain. Too many obstacles stand in your way, such as the basket strainer on a kitchen sink, the pop-up assembly on a bathroom sink, or the drain assembly on a bathtub.

To clear a sluggish or stopped sink, remove your sink trap. After checking that the tailpiece and trap are clear of debris, insert a plumbing auger into the drainpipe. If the trap arm is too low to get the auger in, remove the trap arm before you start.

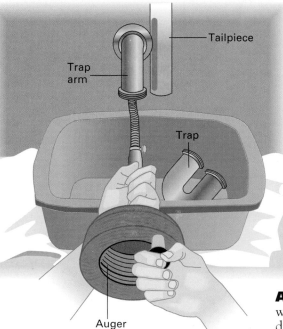

Tailpiece

Trap arm

Trap

Auger

On sinks, you'll have to dismantle the trap (see page 16). Place a dishpan or bucket under the trap, with a drop cloth to catch splashes. You'll also want a drop cloth on the floor.

For a bath drain, the straightest shot is usually through the overflow tube (see page 31). Remove the drain assembly (see pages 30–31) before inserting the auger.

AUGERING TECHNIQUE: Loosen the setscrew on the auger, and push the cable into the drain until it stops. Tighten the setscrew so that you have about 6 inches of cable between the auger and the pipe; if you have too much cable exposed, it will kink while you crank.

Turn the crank clockwise while pushing with medium pressure. If it suddenly starts moving forward, you have gotten past a bend or other fitting. Loosen the setscrew, push the cable as far as it will go, keeping the same distance from the pipe, tighten the setscrew, and crank again. Repeat these steps until you reach the clog.

The auger may push the obstruction through, or it may grab the stuff. If the cranking gets hard, pull the cable out and clean away any solid matter from the auger's tip. If the drain does not run freely, repeat.

AUGERING A TOILET: A toilet auger has a long handle with a crank, and a plastic sleeve at the bend so the cable won't scratch the toilet. Pull the handle all the way up and insert the auger into the toilet. Crank clockwise and push forward. The auger may push the obstruction through. If you feel the auger grabbing something, pull it out but test the toilet as you would if you had plunged it.

The auger won't grab some solid objects, such as children's toy action figures, so if the toilet continues to flush sluggishly or overflow after plunging and augering, you will have to remove the toilet to reach the object (see pages 64–65).

PUSHING THE BLOCKAGE THROUGH: In places where it is difficult to auger, consider blasting the blockage through. Buy an aerosol blockage remover and follow the package instructions. Block off all openings and push on the can to generate force.

A simple garden hose can generate quite a bit of pressure. Use it with a pressurized device like the one shown below, or shove the hose in as far as it will go and seal off the opening with wet rags. Have a helper turn on the spigot while you hold everything tightly in position. If the blockage clears, you will hear the hose run freely.

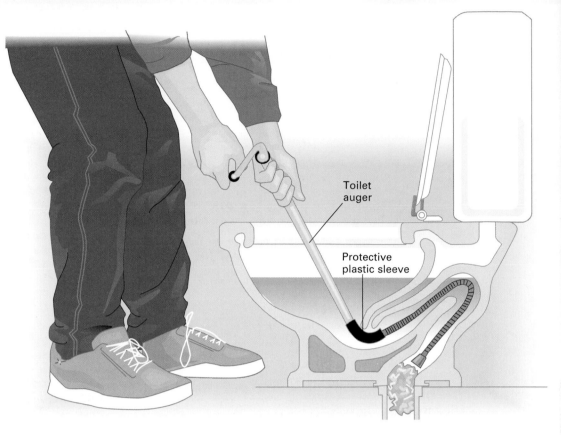

Toilet auger

Protective plastic sleeve

To auger a toilet, pull on the auger's handle to retract the cable. Set the bent end in place and turn the crank as you push the cable.

If you do not have a pressurized device like this one, try shoving the hose in as far as it will go and then stuff rags around the hose to seal the joint. Turn on the water full blast to push out a blockage.

ADJUSTING A TUB DRAIN ASSEMBLY

Every now and then the problem with a tub drain is not that it's clogged; it's that it won't stop running. It's time for some adjustments. There are three basic types of tub drain assemblies: plunger, pop-up, and lift-and-drain. All are designed to be repaired and replaced from inside the tub so you don't need to open the access panel in the wall or cut an opening for a new access panel.

A PLUNGER ASSEMBLY has a brass plunger that slides up and down the overflow pipe as the lever is moved. When the plunger is down, it seals the assembly at the drain.

A POP-UP TUB DRAIN is more complicated and works much the same way as a pop-up assembly for a bathroom sink (*see opposite and page 38*). The control lever at the overflow is attached to a linkage running down the overflow pipe. When the handle is pulled up, a coiled spring at the bottom of the linkage pushes down on a rocker arm and raises the stopper.

A LIFT-AND-DRAIN ASSEMBLY is the simplest and the easiest to fix and install. It has no mechanism in either the drainpipe or the overflow pipe. Instead, there is a toe-operated plug at the drain opening. In some models you lift and twist to open the drain; in other models, you flip a lever.

When removing tub assemblies, it is all too easy to lose small parts down the drain. Save yourself from such aggravation—cover the drain as soon as you can with a rag.

(If you suspect that your tub drain is leaking, check an adjoining room or closet for an access panel that will let you inspect for leaks and make needed repairs. Without this panel, you may have to cut into the wall behind the tub.)

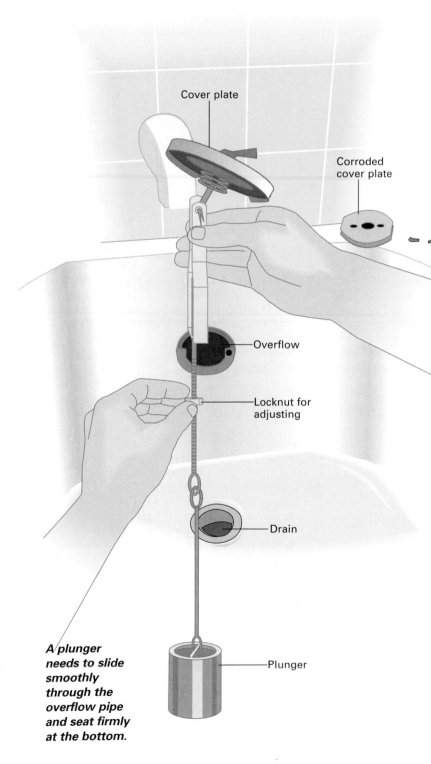

Cover plate

Corroded cover plate

Overflow

Locknut for adjusting

Drain

Plunger

A plunger needs to slide smoothly through the overflow pipe and seat firmly at the bottom.

PLUNGER ASSEMBLY

If your bathtub has no stopper in the drain, you have a plunger assembly. Remove the screws from the cover plate on the overflow opening, and gently pull the pieces up and out. The linkage will be attached to the cover plate. Take care not to bend it—there's no need to pull hard. Remove any gunk and debris, and clean the parts. Lubricate the plunger with heatproof grease and slide it back in. Test the assembly to see if the tub holds water when the lever is pulled up.

If the water still drains, try adjusting the plunger. Adjust the locknut on the lift rod up so that the plunger can travel farther down.

If the drain still does not hold water, the parts may be worn. Replacing the plunger may solve the problem, but chances are good that the plunger seat in the pipe is also worn. Replace the whole assembly, or install a lift-and-drain assembly.

A toe-type tub drain is pulled up or down with your toe and requires no linkage.

LIFT-AND-DRAIN ASSEMBLY

To repair a lift-and-drain assembly or to install one as a replacement for a plunger or pop-up assembly, buy a lift-and-drain kit. It will allow you to install a toe-latch assembly working entirely from inside the tub.

Remove the innards of the existing assembly. To unscrew the drain piece, insert the handles of standard pliers into the strainer holes. Put a ring of plumber's putty under the flange of the drain piece and screw the replacement drain piece back in.

If the drainpipe falls down so you cannot screw the new piece in, have a helper hold it up while you work. Then install the kit and reattach the overflow cover.

POP-UP ASSEMBLY

To remove a pop-up assembly for replacement or repairs, pull the lever up to raise the

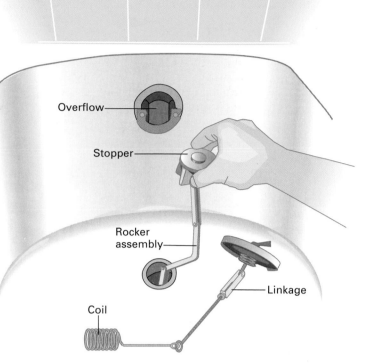

Remove a pop-up assembly by pulling the stopper and rocker assembly out of the drain and the linkage out of the overflow.

stopper. Pull the stopper and the rocker arm out of the opening, taking care not to bend any parts. Clean away any debris. Next, remove the cover plate, and pull out the linkage and spring. To adjust, loosen the locknut so the spring allows the stopper to seat completely. If it still does not hold water completely, the stopper or the drain opening may be nicked or worn. In that case, buy replacement parts or replace the pop-up with a lift-and-drain assembly.

DRUM TRAPS

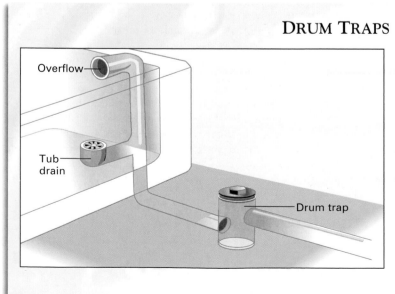

Many older bathrooms have drum traps instead of P-traps for the bathtub. These have a round cover, usually chrome-plated, on the floor near the tub. If you can't get it loose with a wrench, try tapping it with a screwdriver and hammer. Don't worry about damaging the cap; it can be replaced. If the threads inside the trap are damaged, buy a cap with a rubber gasket that expands to fit snugly when you tighten down on a nut.

If the trap is full of water, insert an auger in the hole leading from the tub to the main drain. If it is only partly full, remove the obstruction between the tub and trap.

PIPE REPAIRS

When serious leaks occur, immediately shut off the water supply to the house (*see page 7*); repairing water damage can be very expensive. Then find the origin of the leak. Sometimes you'll be able to see water coming out of an exposed pipe, but more often you'll have to do some damp detective work.

Because water can travel along joists and other surfaces before emerging, the leak may originate several yards from where it appears. You may have to remove access panels and even cut into a wall or ceiling to pinpoint the source.

If water is leaking down from a bathroom, the plumbing may not be at fault. If someone taking a shower forgot to put the curtain inside the tub, the water that splashed onto the floor can leak into the room below. Even small gaps in caulking or tile grout can allow a surprising amount of water to escape into areas where you don't want it.

If a plumbing leak is intermittent, it may come from a drainpipe that carries water only when the sink, tub, or fixture is being used. Or the problem may be located between the fixture valve and spout, showing up only after the valve has been opened. However, if the problem is constant, suspect a supply pipe.

PLUMBER'S EPOXY

For leaks at joints, where you can't fit a pipe clamp or dresser coupling, use epoxy for a temporary repair.

Plumber's epoxy comes in a claylike ribbon of two portions, each a different color. Cut off a piece of the ribbon, and knead it until the two parts are completely mixed to a uniform color. You'll have to shut off the water and dry the area if the leak is serious, though you can work wet if you only have a drip. Push the epoxy around the joint until you have a tight seal.

TEMPORARY RELIEF

Once you've found the source of the leak, the best repair is to remove and replace it. However, sometimes you need a quick temporary solution.

If the leak is on a straight pipe and you have access to it, use a pipe clamp. Remove burrs around the leak to avoid piercing the clamp's rubber gasket. Center the gasket over the hole. Place the clamp pieces around the gasket and tighten the screws or nuts. A clamp like this can last several years.

DRESSER COUPLING

A dresser coupling is considered a permanent solution, but it should be used only where the pipe is left exposed—never hide a dresser coupling behind a wall. Shut off the water and cut through the pipe at the leak. On each side of the cut, slide on a nut, retainer, and gasket. Then center the coupling body over the cut. Apply pipe joint compound or Teflon tape to the body threads and tighten the nuts.

Don't bother making a temporary repair to a fixture trap. Just put a bucket under the trap, minimize use of the sink, and get the replacement parts as soon as possible.

Stainless steel repair clamp

Most leaks occur at fittings; but when a pipe fractures from a dent, corrosion, or freezing, repair it with a clamp (above) or a dresser coupling (right).

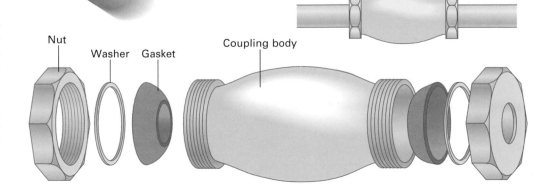

Nut
Washer   Gasket
Coupling body

INCREASING WATER PRESSURE

What seems to be a serious problem—reduced water pressure to one or more faucets—may turn out to be an easy repair. Low pressure is most common in older homes with galvanized steel pipes, which become clogged with minerals and rust.

AERATORS AND SHOWERHEADS

An aerator, attached at the tip of a spout, contains tiny passages that mix air with the water. Aerated water doesn't splash so much when it hits the sink, but its tiny passages are easily clogged.

If you can't remove an aerator by hand, use tongue-and-groove pliers and a protective cloth. Pay attention to the order and position of the internal parts as you remove them. Typically, the screen is clogged with light-colored mineral flecks or rust. Use a pin or a toothbrush to unclog it. If the screen is badly clogged, replace it.

Showerheads should be removed and cleaned every year or so. Again, use tongue-and-groove pliers and a protective cloth, and pay attention to how the pieces go together. Soak the parts in vinegar overnight. If the perforations remain clogged, replace the screen.

OTHER CULPRITS

If clearing an aerator does not restore flow, remove it, turn on the faucet, and repeatedly shut and open the stop valves as rapidly as possible. This may loosen rust and sediment,

CLEARING GALVANIZED PIPES

In some areas where old galvanized piping is common, you can find companies that specialize in cleaning out sediment to improve water pressure.

One method involves disconnecting the home's water supply and hooking up a hose to a pipe near the top of the house. Water is flushed through the pipes backwards, which clears out a fair amount of the buildup.

A more thorough professional technique takes months of chemically treating the pipes. During the treatment, you will often need to clean loosened sludge from aerators, faucets, and valves. A leak or two may appear as well, because mineral deposits fill what would otherwise be leaks. At the end of the treatment, the insides of the pipes will be like new.

which will then come out of the spout.

If that also fails, shut off water to the house, and remove the shutoff valves and sink-supply lines (risers). Clean out the incoming water lines with a long screwdriver or unbent clothes hanger. Put buckets under the pipes and turn water back on for a few seconds, to flush the pipes. Flush out the risers and shutoff valves before reinstalling them.

Some types of faucets get clogged easily if sediment enters them. If water flows freely out of the risers but not out of the faucet, follow the instructions on pages 40–49 to disassemble the faucet. Clean out any particles and reinstall.

WASHING MACHINE: The usual cause of reduced flow to a washing machine is buildup of sediment in the strainers, which are located just inside the hot and cold hose connections on the back of the machine. Detach the hose couplings and clean or replace the screens.

CHECK PIPE SIZES: If pressure is low throughout the house, check the size of the pipe at the house shutoff valve. It should be at least ¾ inch. A cold-water pipe should continue at a minimum diameter of ¾ inch all the way to the water heater. If this pipe is ½ inch, replacing it with a ¾-inch pipe may solve low flow throughout the house. Doing the same with pipes coming out of the water heater can also improve pressure.

Cleaning a showerhead will make you a household hero in exchange for only a few minutes of work.

Most aerators can be removed by hand and cleaned with a toothpick, pin, or old toothbrush.

QUIETING PIPES

Noisy pipes are usually just an annoyance, but rattling supply lines may develop leaks at the joints. Here's how to silence the rumblings.

Shock absorber

Add shock absorbers to your system to eliminate water hammer. They hold air in a chamber to cushion the shocks when water is turned off and on.

Ferrule

Compression nut

WATER HAMMER

Knocking and rattling of water lines, known as water hammer, is caused by shock waves sent through the pipes when fast-moving water rapidly shuts down. Common sources include appliances with electronic shutoff valves, such as dishwashers and washing machines, and single-handle faucets on tubs and showers.

To find the knocking pipe, have a helper turn an appliance or faucet on and off quickly to cause the sound while you pinpoint the location of the noise.

Wrap the guilty pipes with foam insulation (sold in 8-foot lengths, sliced lengthwise so you can install them quickly) and add hangers to hold the pipes firm. Wherever possible, eliminate contact between pipes and wood.

Another way to eliminate water hammer is to install an air chamber, also called a shock absorber. This simple and inexpensive device contains an air chamber or a flexible diaphragm to dampen the shock wave. To install one, you will need to cut into the pipe and install a tee.

OTHER CREEPY NOISES

When water pressure entering a house is too high (most codes set a limit of 80 pounds per square inch), you may hear a variety of shrieks and moans as well as hammering. High pressure does more than make noise—it also can damage electronic shutoffs in appliances. Have your pressure checked by your water supplier. If high pressure is the problem, install a pressure-reducing valve. Check the incoming water line just downstream of the house shutoff to see if you already have a pressure-reducing valve that no longer works. Replace it, or if you don't have one, install one near the water meter.

A chattering or rattling that comes on when you barely turn on a faucet is probably due to a defective seat washer. Repair the faucet (*see pages 40–49*).

If you hear noises when a dishwasher starts, the problem is probably a worn-out dishwasher pump; have the pump replaced.

LOUD DRAIN LINES

Older homes used cast-iron drainpipes, which effectively muffled the sound of water running through them. If your plastic drainpipes annoy you with the noise every time you flush a toilet, wrap them with foam or fiberglass insulation.

Copper supply pipes are especially liable to vibrate and hammer. Clamp them tightly so they can't vibrate, and use foam insulation to cushion them.

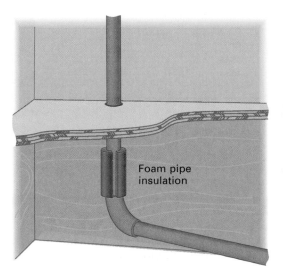

Foam pipe insulation

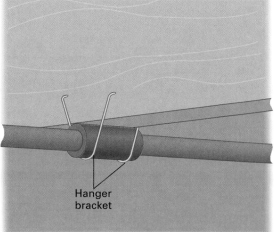

Hanger bracket

SHUTOFF VALVES

Your supply system will have several kinds of shutoff valves. The main shutoff controls the water for the whole house. Secondary shutoffs let you turn off water in sections of the stem. Both main and secondary valves are available in a variety of sizes. Some screw onto galvanized pipes, and others are designed to be soldered onto copper pipe.

GATE VALVE

This old-style valve is not very reliable. A wedge-shaped brass gate slides up and down when you turn the handle. When the gate becomes worn, it won't seal. There is no rubber part to replace. Replace the gate or, better yet, the entire valve. If it leaks only around the packing nut, replace the strand packing or install a packing washer.

GLOBE VALVE

This valve uses a stem washer to seal water off, much like a compression faucet (see page 40). If it doesn't shut off the water completely, replace the stem washer. If there is a leak around the packing nut, replace the packing washer or, in an older model, twist packing string under the nut around the stem.

NURSING AN OLD VALVE

An older home may have a main shutoff valve that is just hanging on. After serving for decades as the gateway for millions of gallons of water, the internal parts are bound to be worn. The best solution is to replace the valve, but sometimes it is difficult to shut the water off prior to the valve; you may have to call the water supplier.

If an old valve does not shut water off completely, try this: Open a faucet that is lower than the pipe or fixture you are working on. The trickle of water will come out of the lower faucet, not your repair. If there is no lower faucet, you'll just have to use buckets under your repair and resign yourself to getting wet.

Some old valves leak at the packing nut when you open or shut them. Try tightening the nut with tongue-and-groove pliers—don't crank down on it with a pipe wrench, or you may crack it.

BALL VALVE

This is more expensive than other valves, but it is very reliable and makes it easy to shut off water quickly. Instead of having a handle that must be turned a number of times, it has a lever that rotates a spherical gate, turning the water on or off with a quarter turn.

If you're doing repairs in an old house with galvanized pipes, turning the water off and on will dislodge rust and mineral deposits. These particles quickly migrate to your faucets. Remove aerators and let the water flow freely for a few seconds to flush out the gunk.

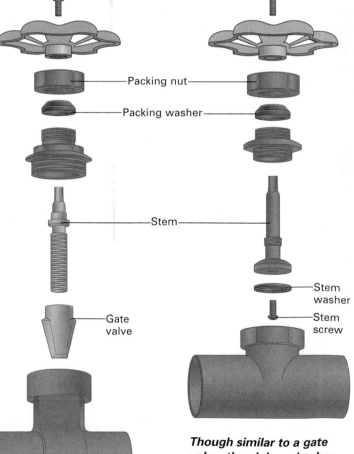

Gate valves have a replaceable packing washer. However, if the gate is worn, it is nearly impossible to replace; install a new valve.

Though similar to a gate valve, the globe valve has replaceable packing and stem washers.

SERVICING RADIATORS

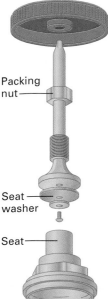

Packing nut—

Seat washer—

Seat—

Both steam and hot-water radiators have release valves, and both systems can have an inlet and outlet pipe (although some steam radiators use one pipe for both functions). Servicing both kinds is similar.

REPAIRS

Remove or disassemble a steam valve when the radiator is cool. Drain a hot-water system before working on it.

FIXING A HANDLE: Remove a cracked or broken handle by unscrewing the setscrew. Take the handle to a home center for replacement. If the threads in the stem are stripped, buy a universal handle that clamps onto the stem.

LEAK NEAR THE PACKING NUT: This problem, common to both systems, often goes undetected because water dribbles down through the floor, causing serious damage over time. Tighten the packing nut or remove the handle and the nut (the water has to be drained if it's a hot-water radiator), and wrap the stem with strand packing.

LEAK AT THE INLET: If water drips from the pipes on either side of the valve, tighten the large nuts at the joint. If this does not solve the problem, the valve or the nut may be cracked and will have to be replaced.

MAINTENANCE

BLEEDING A HOT-WATER RADIATOR: If a hot-water radiator isn't heating to full capacity, it may need to have trapped air bled away. (Bleed all your radiators, or at least those on the top floor, every year to ensure maximum output.) Put a cup or a bucket under the bleeder valve and open it slowly. If air is present, it will hiss or sputter. Once water starts flowing freely (be careful, it's hot), close the valve.

STEAM RADIATOR VENTS: A steam radiator with only one pipe at the bottom has a small vent, usually chrome-plated, near the top at the end and opposite the valve. This vent releases steam only at the end of a heating cycle. If yours steams whenever the radiator is on, it should be replaced. Unscrew the vent and take it to a plumbing-supply source for replacement.

Sometimes these vents break off, making it impossible to unscrew what's left in the hole. If this happens, drill the broken stem out using a bit slightly smaller than the opening. Then use a radiator vent tool to tap out the hole. The tool creates new threads as you screw the vent in.

Steam radiators cannot be turned down by partially closing the valve; the valve must be completely open or completely closed. If you want to make a radiator less hot, purchase an adjustable vent. Install it as you would any vent, by screwing it in. Adjust the heat by turning a knob or screwdriver slot on the adjustable vent.

The steam or hot-water valve on a radiator uses a simple compression stem with a replaceable seat and seat washer. If you find a leak at the packing nut, tighten it or wrap the shaft with strand packing.

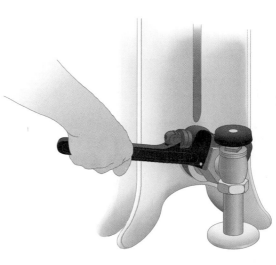

WINTERIZING AND DEFROSTING PIPES

Waking up to water lines that have frozen solid during the night is not only annoying but worrisome. Because water expands when it freezes, it may fracture a pipe or valve. If your pipes freeze, you need to restore flow and check for leaks.

PREVENTING FREEZE-UPS

If your house has a history of frozen pipes and you haven't insulated them yet, you can still take stop-gap steps when cold weather is on the way. Fill a tub full of water, shut off the house water for the night, drain the system by opening the lowest faucet, and sleep soundly: The pipes will not freeze, the tub will give you water to use the next morning, and each toilet in the house will be good for one flush.

If freeze-ups occur only in certain pipes, a less radical precaution is to let a faucet run slowly all night. Water moving through a pipe is less likely to freeze than still water.

HEAT TAPE: Sooner or later, you'll need a more thorough solution. Wrap pipes with electric pipe-heating tape. Because it is thermostatically controlled, pipe-heating tape uses power only when needed. However, it will not work during a power outage.

INSULATION: Once you have determined which pipes tend to freeze, wrap them with foam insulation if you can get at them. If the pipes are hidden in a wall, insulate the wall with blown-in foam or cellulose.

WINTERIZING A HOUSE

If you plan to leave a house unoccupied during winter months, shut off the water supply and drain the system by opening the lowest faucet. Flush the toilets. If any of your valves have drain cocks, open them. Open every faucet. Crack open any unions.

Pour a mixture of automotive antifreeze and water (see the container for the ratio) into toilet bowls and all fixtures with traps—sinks, showers, and washing-machine standpipes. When you return, shut all the faucets, reattach all unions, and close any drain cocks. Turn on the main water supply, and then start turning on faucets, beginning at the bottom of the system and working up.

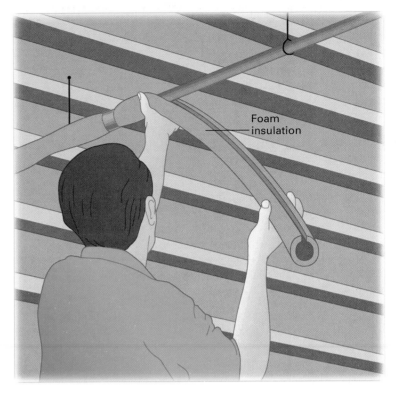

Foam insulation

Freeze-prone pipes can be insulated easily with commercial foam wraps.

DEFROSTING PIPES

If your pipes are frozen and you aren't able to thaw them immediately, you may have to just shut off the water and let the ice melt as the day warms up. Then turn the water back on and check for leaks.

To thaw pipes safely, use a hair dryer or a heat gun designed for stripping paint. If the pipes are concealed in a wall, open a faucet and aim a space heater at the wall. If you leave the house, turn off the faucet.

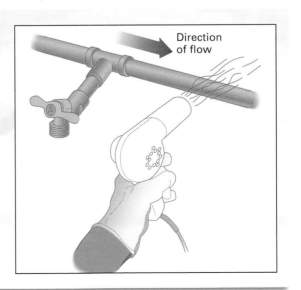

Direction of flow

*Most bathroom sinks (also called basins or lavatories)
have supply and drain assemblies that are inexpensive
and easy to repair.*

COMMON REPAIRS

After clearing clogs and improving pressure, most other do-it-yourself plumbing chores involve stopping drips and replacing old fixtures. This chapter covers common plumbing repairs, all of which you can easily complete in a weekend. None of them involves running new plumbing lines. Very likely, the most time-consuming aspect of these repairs will be the trips to the hardware or plumbing-supply store to get the right parts.

A dribbling sink or tub faucet not only wastes water, its drip-drip-dripping strains your peace of mind and stains your fixtures. While four basic types of valves are used in most faucets (see pages 40–49), there are scores, if not hundreds, of variations of each. If your faucet is old or unusual, you may have difficulty finding parts and have to replace the entire faucet. Or, you may be tempted to replace the faucet supply because you want a new style. If you do so, avoid the inexpensive units made of plastic and pot metal: They can chip, flake, and corrode within months.

Follow the sequence of steps for diagnosing and repairing problems. Keep track of all the parts—in some cases, there will be quite a few small pieces, all of which are necessary. Having leftover parts after reassembling does not mean you are a marvel of efficiency—it means something isn't going to work. And keep everything clean while you work: Even a little dirt in the wrong place can cause leaks or damage fittings.

If you need to purchase a new sink or toilet, you'll find that basic porcelain fixtures can be surprisingly inexpensive, though cheaper sinks tend to be downscaled, and less-expensive toilets will have lower-quality mechanical parts.

REPAIRING A POP-UP ASSEMBLY

The picture (*left*) shows a typical pop-up drain assembly for a bathroom sink. These assemblies are nearly universal; so if yours has bent or worn parts, you can purchase replacements that will fit. Some stoppers rest on top of the pivot rod and rely on their own weight and a thin gasket to make a tight seal. Other stoppers have a slot or loop that fits over the end of the pivot rod to pull the stopper down onto its sealing surface.

If the stopper does not completely seal, or if it does not rise up high enough, check the linkage first. The clevis screw may have come loose. To make the mechanism run smoothly, you may need to adjust the height of the clevis or move the spring clip so the clevis is straight up and down.

If the pivot rod nut leaks, try tightening it, which will cause more friction when you raise and lower the stopper. If that doesn't solve the problem, get a new pivot rod.

COMPRESSION-STEM FAUCETS

Kitchen, bathroom, and shower faucets come in four basic designs: compression-stem, cartridge, disk, and ball. The following pages give general instructions for repairing all of them. Because each type has many variations, your faucet may not look exactly like those illustrated. Go to your hardware dealer with the brand name of your faucet, as well as some of its parts, to find exact replacement parts.

Of the many styles of faucet valves, compression-stem faucets have the most variety. This design, which uses separate handles for hot and cold water, has been made by many manufacturers for over a century, so there are thousands of configurations.

Decorative cap

Screw

Handle

Packing nut

Stem

Packing washer

Seat washer

Washer screw

Valve seat

Compression stems come in many different sizes and shapes. Some are very long, and others are stubby. All have washers at the end, which fit into seats in the faucet body to stop the flow of water.

Compression stem

FIXING A STEM LEAK

Shut the water off at the main or fixture shutoff valves and open the faucet until the water drains from the line. Cover the drain so small parts cannot fall into it.

REMOVING THE HANDLE: Pry off the decorative cap with a table knife or a small screwdriver and loosen the screw that holds the handle. Sometimes you can pull off the handle easily, but often it sticks. Rock it back and forth while pulling up. Often the handle has a splined recess that fits tightly down over matching splines on the stem. If the handle is so tight that you need to pry it off with a screwdriver, use a thin piece of wood to protect the sink or the faucet body. For stubborn or corroded handles, use a faucet-handle puller *right*. (You may have to replace the handles, but at least you'll get them off.)

REMOVING PACKING NUT AND STEM: Once you get the handles off, you'll see the packing nut, which holds the stem in the faucet body. If your leak is only at the stem, remove the packing nut and remove the packing—either a domed washer or wound Teflon or graphite. Replace the packing nut and the handles.

FIXING A DRIPPING FAUCET

A compression-stem faucet can leak from the spout because of a worn washer or a damaged seat, or the stem itself may be damaged. Follow the steps above to remove the handles and packing nut. Then use a pliers or the faucet handle (put it back loosely on the splines) to unscrew the stem.

REPLACING A WASHER: If the washer is pitted or ripped, it cannot seal completely. Unscrew the brass screw that holds the washer on the end of the stem. You may have to use a knife to remove the washer, but do not damage the retainer.

Find a replacement washer that is exactly the same size as the old one. A beveled washer will reduce water pressure somewhat, but it can provide a watertight seal if the seat is somewhat uneven and corroded. You also may need to replace the brass screw that holds the washer in place.

REPAIRING OR REPLACING A SEAT: While you have the stem out, check the valve seat for damage. Poke your finger down into the faucet body and feel it. If it is rough,

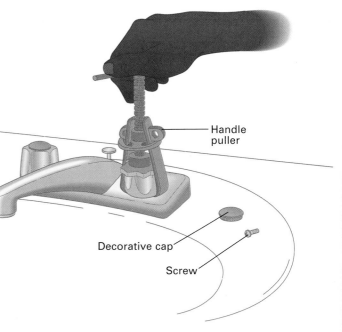

Handle puller

Decorative cap

Screw

1. Faucet handles often can't be removed by rocking them back and forth while prying with a screwdriver. An inexpensive handle puller does the job easily.

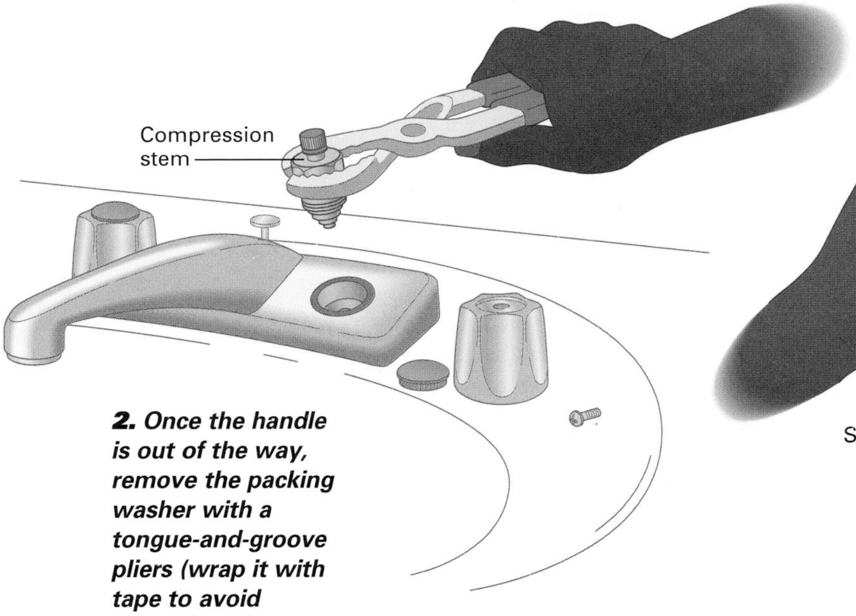

Compression
stem

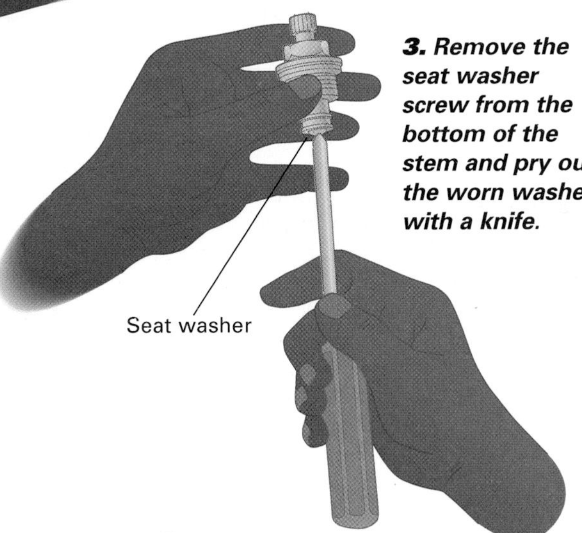

3. *Remove the seat washer screw from the bottom of the stem and pry out the worn washer with a knife.*

Seat washer

2. *Once the handle is out of the way, remove the packing washer with a tongue-and-groove pliers (wrap it with tape to avoid damaging the stem). Then unscrew the stem.*

O-ring

it will quickly damage a new washer. In this case you have two options: Use a stem wrench, which is like an allen wrench, to remove and replace the valve seat; or grind the seat smooth using a seat-grinding tool.

REINSTALLING THE STEM: Apply a generous coat of heatproof plumber's grease to the stem threads before twisting the stem back into the faucet body. Leave the stem in the open position before you tighten the packing nut so the new washer is not overtightened into the seat.

If you haven't already done so, replace the packing washer or wind enough strand packing tightly around the stem that you can start the packing nut by hand. You may need a few tries to get the right amount.

If a new washer and a new or smoothed seat do not fix the leak, the stem itself may be damaged. If a replacement stem is not available, replace the faucet.

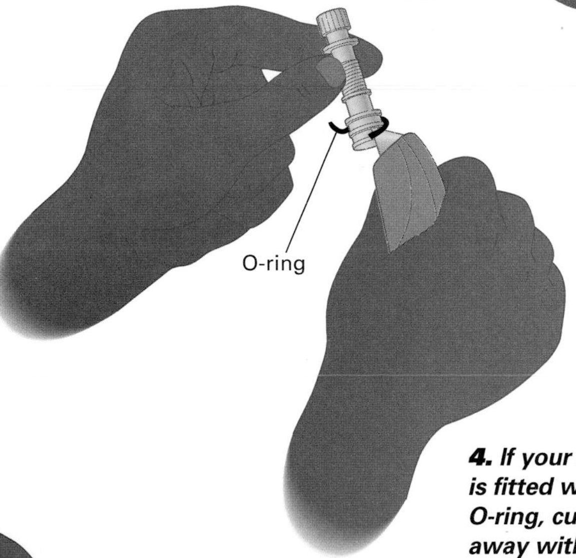

4. *If your stem is fitted with an O-ring, cut it away with a utility knife. Try not to scratch the stem.*

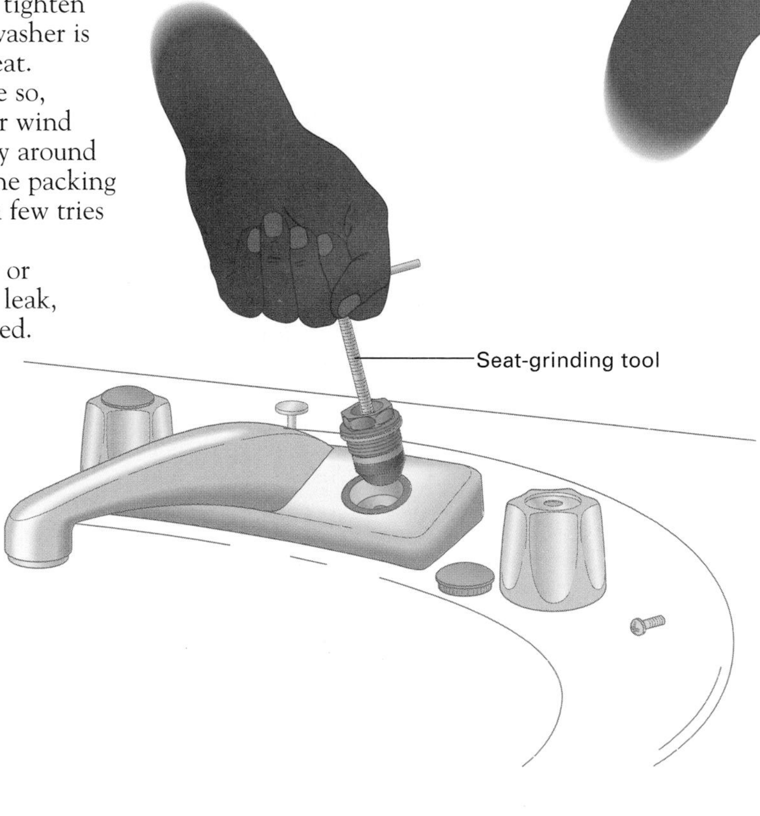

Seat-grinding tool

5. *A stem-grinding tool screws into the faucet body to help you grind evenly. Push gently, rotate two or three times, and test the seat with your finger to see if it is smooth.*

DIAPHRAGM- AND CARTRIDGE-STEM FAUCETS

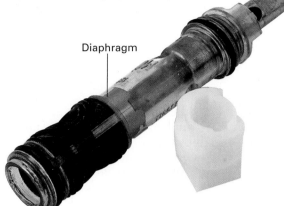

Diaphragm

Diaphragm stems (also called top-hat stems) work in a way similar to compression-stem faucets but use a neoprene diaphragm to seal against a seat instead of a washer.

Individual cartridge stems work much the same way as single-handle cartridges (*see pages 48–49*), but there are two cartridges—one for hot water and one for cold water, and each has only a single water inlet.

Repairing each of these stems is easy, but it may be difficult to find the parts. Take the stem with you to a home center or plumbing-supply store to get an exact match.

DIAPHRAGM STEM: Shut off the water and drain the faucet. Remove the handle as you would a compression-stem faucet (*see page 40*), and pull out the stem. Pry a worn diaphragm off and slip on a new one. Check the seat as you would for a compression faucet (*see page 40*).

CARTRIDGE STEM: Shut off the water and drain the faucet. Cover the sink opening—there are small parts. Pry off the "hot" or "cold" cap and remove the screw holding the handle. Remove the handle and unscrew the plastic retaining ring. Take note of the position of the cartridge so you

can replace it facing the same direction, and pull the cartridge stem straight up with pliers.

Buy a kit containing a new O-ring and a new seal. Use a sharp pencil to pry out the rubber seal at the bottom of the stem—carefully—and a small spring will pop out. Remove the O-ring using your fingernail or a knife. Be careful not to nick the stem.

Set a new spring into the opening, and push in a new seal. Slip on a new O-ring so it seats all the way in the groove. Coat the rubber parts lightly with heatproof plumber's grease and reinstall the stem.

Once you've replaced the O-ring and seal on a cartridge-stem faucet, fit it into the keyways machined into the faucet base.

Key

O-ring

Seal

Keyway

Water inlet

CHICAGO STYLE

The Chicago-style faucet is confusing because it seems to work backwards—the stem moves up to turn water off and down to turn water on. It is actually a variation on the compression stem. Usually you can fix a drip by replacing the washer at the end of the stem. But a standard washer will not work; you have to have a washer designed specifically for this faucet.

TUB AND SHOWER FAUCETS

Shower faucets are essentially the same as sink faucets, only they are larger and are positioned horizontally. Some types have the shower water diverter on the faucet body; others have it on the spout.

To make repairs, first shut off water and drain the line either at the house, the supply line, or if you have them, at built-in shutoff valves under the cover plate. Built-in valves are usually found only in single-handle units; turn them off using a large screwdriver.

Then remove the handles. Be careful when loosening the handle—too much force could damage pipe joints and cause leaks inside the wall. You may need to use a handle puller.

After removing the handle, disassemble the valve and use one of these repair techniques, depending on the type of valve involved.

ONE-HANDLE BALL FAUCET: Openings in the ball allow water to pass through when the ball is rotated or moved up and down. (*See pages 46–47 for information on repairing a ball faucet.*) These small orifices can get clogged, especially with corrosion from galvanized pipes. Remove the ball, clean out all the orifices, and replace any worn parts. If the ball itself is worn, replace it. Take the old parts with you when buying replacements. Many parts look the same, but aren't.

TWO-HANDLE COMPRESSION STEM: These are essentially horizontally mounted compression-stem sink faucets. Replace the packing washer or strands if the handle leaks, and replace the seat washer if the faucet drips. (*See pages 40–41.*) Seats in these units often wear out. If your seat is worn, a new washer will soon leak again. If it feels rough, use a seat wrench to extract the seat, and replace it.

THREE-HANDLE COMPRESSION STEM: This is like its two-handled cousin with the addition of a diverter valve in the middle. Repair the outer valves using the same method as for a two-handle unit. If the diverter doesn't do its job, or if it sticks, remove it as you would a regular stem. Disassemble it and replace any rubber parts, or replace the whole diverter stem.

ONE-HANDLE CARTRIDGE: There are many types of cartridges, so buy a repair kit made by the manufacturer of your faucet before disassembling. The parts may all be plastic, so work carefully and don't nick any of them; often it is easier to replace the entire cartridge rather than just the O-rings. Take note of the cartridge orientation as you remove it; if you put it back the wrong way, hot and cold will be reversed.

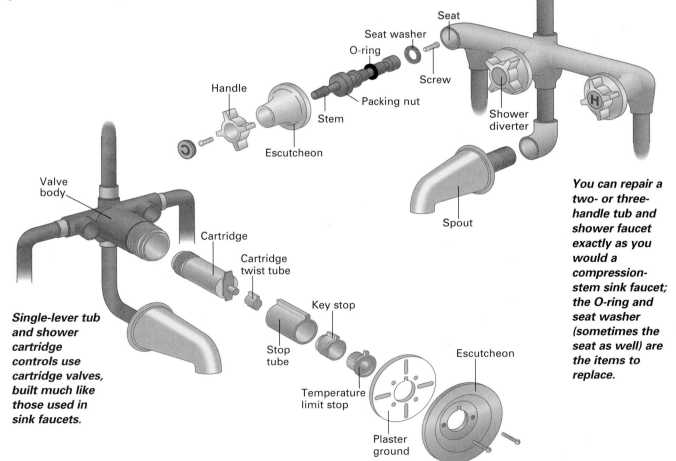

Single-lever tub and shower cartridge controls use cartridge valves, built much like those used in sink faucets.

You can repair a two- or three-handle tub and shower faucet exactly as you would a compression-stem sink faucet; the O-ring and seat washer (sometimes the seat as well) are the items to replace.

DISK FAUCETS

A disk faucet has two plastic or ceramic disks, an upper one that can be rotated and a lower stationary disk. Both disks are housed in a cylinder that is located just under the handle.

The rotating disk is controlled by the action of the handle and has openings that align with water inlets (one for hot, the other for cold) in the fixed disk. When the handle is turned so that the holes line up with the inlets, water is allowed to flow to the spout; when the openings are rotated off the inlets, water is cut off.

Disk faucets depend on replaceable neoprene seals—usually set into the fixed disk at the bottom of the cylinder—to ensure a seal. If water drips out of the spout or wells up around the top of the faucet when it is in use, the seals need to be replaced.

DISASSEMBLE

Shut off the water and turn on the faucet until water stops running. To remove the handle, locate the small setscrew, usually on the lower front surface. (Unfortunately, it's sometimes on the rear of the handle.) Use a small-blade screwdriver or an allen wrench to loosen the setscrew, and pull the handle from the connecting rod that extends upward from the rotating disk.

Use tongue-and-groove pliers wrapped in tape to unscrew the dome housing (also called an escutcheon cap).

Remove the cylinder assembly by unscrewing two or three mounting screws.

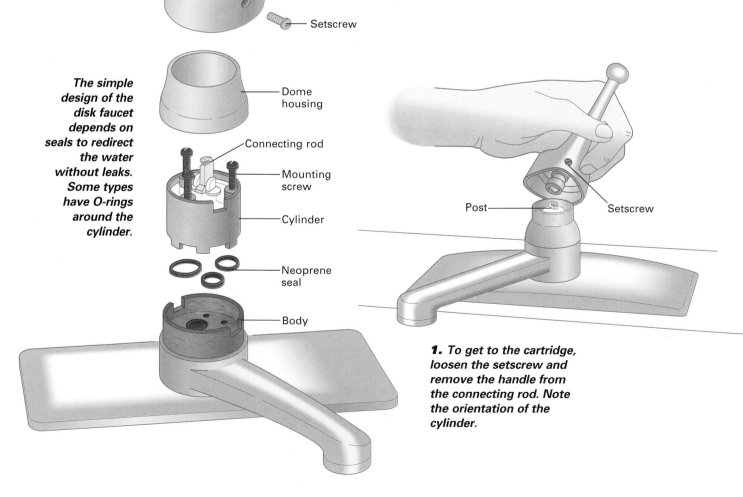

The simple design of the disk faucet depends on seals to redirect the water without leaks. Some types have O-rings around the cylinder.

1. *To get to the cartridge, loosen the setscrew and remove the handle from the connecting rod. Note the orientation of the cylinder.*

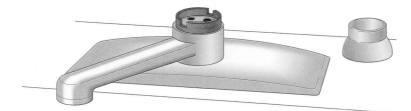

2. *Remove the dome housing, unfasten the three mounting screws, and pull out the cylinder. Clean the outside of the body and make sure there are no particles in any of the orifices.*

Disk assembly

Seals

3. *Gently remove the neoprene seals and, if your faucet has them, fine wire mesh filter cones.*

CLEAN AND REPLACE SEALS

Remove the neoprene seals with your fingernail or pry them out carefully with a small screwdriver, taking care not to nick the area around them. There may be small filter cones made of fine wire mesh; remove them as well.

Ceramic disks rarely need to be replaced, but plastic disks and their cylinder may wear out and have to be replaced. If the disk seals do not look worn, you may get by without replacing them. Use a toothbrush or non-metallic scouring pad to clean away all particles and sludge from the inlet holes and filter cones and clean the seals thoroughly.

Replace the old seals or install new ones made by the manufacturer. Be sure the seals seat completely in their orifices.

Slip the cylinder back in, oriented in the same direction as it was originally. Anchor it with the mounting screws and screw the dome housing back on. Reinstall the handle by tightening the setscrew.

Restore water pressure and test for water flow and leaks. If the faucet still leaks, replace the cylinder.

4. *Clean the inlet holes. Small pieces of debris will not only inhibit water flow, they can cause leaks if they get caught in the seals.*

5. *Reinsert the old seals if they aren't worn, or replace them with new ones made by the manufacturer.*

Mounting screws

6. *Replace the cylinder and fasten the mounting screws.*

BALL FAUCETS

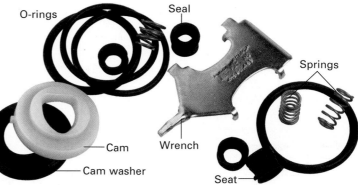

O-rings

Seal

Springs

Cam

Wrench

Cam washer

Seat

Called a rotating ball faucet or a Delta faucet (after one of its manufacturers), this type has a smooth plastic or metal ball that rotates in a socket in the faucet body. As the ball rotates with the movement of the handle, grooves in the ball pass over or away from water inlet valve seats.

If you have a leak at the spout or at the handle, first tighten the dome housing or adjusting ring with tongue-and-groove pliers (use a rag or add tape to the plier jaws to prevent

scratching the chrome). Use medium force. If that doesn't work, disassemble the faucet and replace worn parts.

Buy a rebuild kit. It will contain all the parts you need, as well as a special tool for removing the handle. A brass ball costs more but lasts longer than a plastic ball.

DISASSEMBLE

Shut off the water and drain the faucet. Loosen the setscrew holding the handle in place. (The rebuild kit may contain a wrench for this screw.) On some models, there is an adjusting ring under the handle; use the special tool from the rebuild kit to unscrew it.

On models without a ring, wrap tape around the jaws of a pair of tongue-and-groove pliers, or use a rag to protect the chrome, and unscrew the cap. Remove the cam and the ball. If the spout turns, remove it as well. You may have to pull hard to get the spout off.

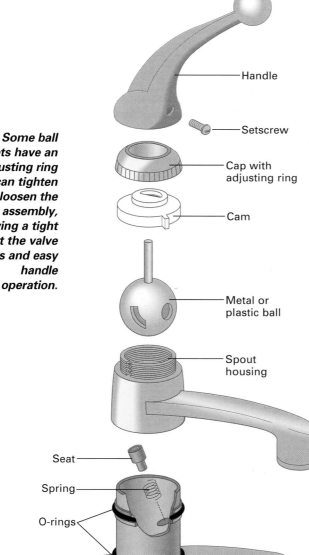

Handle

Setscrew

Cap with adjusting ring

Cam

Metal or plastic ball

Spout housing

Seat

Spring

O-rings

Some ball faucets have an adjusting ring that can tighten or loosen the assembly, allowing a tight seal at the valve seats and easy handle operation.

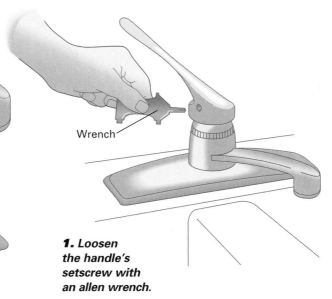

Wrench

1. Loosen the handle's setscrew with an allen wrench.

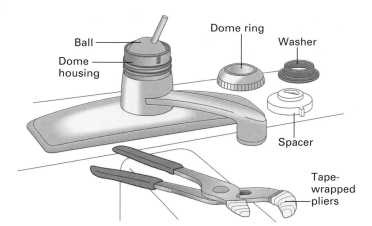

2. *Using tape-wrapped pliers to prevent scratching, unscrew the cap and remove the cam. Some models have a washer and a spacer.*

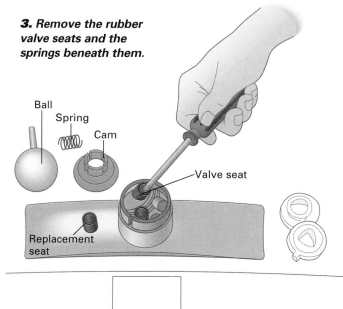

3. *Remove the rubber valve seats and the springs beneath them.*

REPLACE PARTS

Use a screwdriver or needle-nose pliers to gently pluck out the small rubber sleeves (the valve seats) visible in the faucet body cavity. Under these rubber sleeves are tiny springs that push the seats against the ball to form a seal. The seals must be watertight, or water will leak out the spout. Replace the springs so they force the seats more firmly onto the ball.

If water has been leaking from the cylindrical collar of the spout, replace the two O-rings that fit in the grooves on the faucet body. (Even if the collar doesn't leak, you may want to replace the O-ring anyway, now that you have the faucet apart.)

If the faucet has a sprayer, there will be a diverter valve in front of the body (*see page 55*). Remove it and replace its small O-ring.

Rub the O-rings and the inside of the spout where it fits over the O-rings with a little heatproof plumber's grease.

ASSEMBLY

When you reassemble the faucet, notice that the ball has a small tab that fits into a slot on the faucet body. Notice, too, that the cam also fits one way, with a tab that slides into a slot in the faucet body. Screw the housing or the adjusting ring tight enough to prevent leaks but not so tight as to make the faucet difficult to operate. Try hand-tightening first; if it leaks when you restore water power, tighten with pliers until the leak stops. Replace the handle.

4. *If water wells up from the base of the spout or if the spout is loose, remove the spout and cut away the O-rings and replace them with exact duplicates.*

5. *Reassemble the faucet. Experiment with the handle to find how tightly you want the spacer or retainer screwed down.*

CARTRIDGE FAUCETS

A wide variety of manufacturers make faucets with cartridges of many shapes and sizes. In general, a cartridge has interior passageways through which water passes. The cartridge is rotated by a single lever or doorknob-like handle. Depending on how it is rotated, the cartridge then presents its opening to the incoming water and allows it to flow through the spout, mixing the hot and cold according to the position of the handle. The flow stops when the cartridge is rotated again so that an opening no longer faces the water inlet.

The cartridge is equipped with O-rings that seal against the interior of the cartridge body. If they are worn, water will leak out the spout. If you have a model with a spout that swivels, there will be one or more O-rings on the faucet body. If these rings are worn, water will leak from the base of the spout.

Because there are so many models, your cartridge faucet may look much different from the one shown and may have a different O-ring configuration. However, repairs are usually easy—replace the cartridge or the O-ring or both. The most difficult part of the job may be finding the correct replacement parts.

DISASSEMBLE

Shut off the water to the sink and drain the faucet. Use a small screwdriver or table knife to pry off the cover plate on top of the handle. The handle screw is underneath. Remove the screw. Move the handle to the off position and remove it by pulling up.

A cartridge rotates easily in its housing, but on some models, you won't be able to get it out without removing the retaining ring. Remove it with tongue-and-groove pliers.

The cartridge is usually held in place with a horseshoe-shaped retaining clip. Grip it firmly with needle-nose pliers and pull it free of the faucet body. Take note of how you will reinstall it: It must enter the faucet body, slide past the top of the cartridge, and extend through to the other side. Lift the cartridge straight up with pliers to remove it.

Decorative cap

Screw

Handle

Retaining ring

O-rings on the cartridge and the faucet body must be in good condition if the faucet is to seal off water.

Cartridge — O-ring

Spout housing

Retaining clip

O-rings

Handle screw

1. Pry off the cap with a table knife or small screwdriver and unscrew the handle screw.

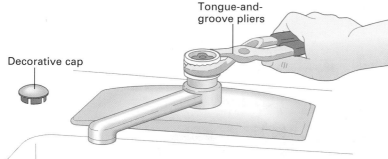

Decorative cap

Tongue-and-groove pliers

2. *If your faucet has a swiveling spout it will have a retaining ring. Under it, you will find a retainer clip that holds the cartridge in place.*

3. *Pull the retaining ring straight up and out, and pull out the retaining clip with needle-nose pliers. Note the position of the cartridge before pulling it out.*

Retaining ring   Cartridge

CLEAN, REPLACE PARTS, AND REINSTALL

If you will be reinstalling the old cartridge, pull out the tubelike strainer in the middle and clean it thoroughly under running water. If the mesh is clogged, clearing it will dramatically increase the flow of water through the faucet. If the mesh is badly clogged, replace the cartridge.

You could try to get by with just replacing the O-rings on the cartridge, but getting the right O-ring may prove difficult. Even if one seems to fit the cartridge, it may not seal tightly against the faucet body. It's usually easier to replace the cartridge. Make sure the replacement cartridge matches the old one exactly; buy one made by the same manufacturer if you can.

Before installing the new or repaired cartridge, apply a light coat of heatproof plumber's grease to all surfaces that move against another. Push the cartridge in firmly, compressing any trapped air, until it hits bottom. Slide the retaining clip all the way in.

On models with swiveling spouts, also replace the large O-ring on the base of the faucet body. Grease it, as well.

Replace the retaining ring (if any). Set the handle on the cartridge stem and install the handle screw. If the handle does not rotate to the positions you want, try again.

4. *If the spout is loose or if water leaks out of its base, cut away O-rings and replace them with duplicates.*

Utility knife

Replacement O-rings

GREASE

5. *Coat a new cartridge with heatproof grease and install it facing the same direction as the old one.*

STOPPING OTHER LEAKS

In addition to fixing internal leaks as described on the previous pages, you may face leaks that develop in and around faucets. The most common fix is replacement of a flawed rubber part. (If this and the remedies discussed on pages 40–49 fail to solve your problem, the best solution may be to replace your faucet, as described on pages 52–53.)

O-rings

SPOUT-BASE LEAKS

If there is a leak at the base of the spout, shut off the water, loosen the swivel nut with tape- or cloth-protected pliers, and remove the spout. Pry up the old O-ring and make sure you have an exact replacement. Coat the new ring with heatproof plumber's grease and install it. Screw the swivel nut hand-tight, then a quarter turn more. If a leak persists after restoring water pressure, tighten the nut slightly.

Fix a leaking spout base by removing the spout and checking the O-rings that seal it.

BASE PLATE SEEPAGE

If you find water in the cabinet under your sink from time to time, first check the trap for leaks (*see page 16*). If the trap is not the source, you may have water coming down through the mounting holes for your base plate.

First try tightening the mounting nuts using a basin wrench (*see page 52*). If that doesn't stop the leaks, the problem may be the putty or gasket under the base plate. Old putty may be hard and cracked, or it may have gaps; the gasket may be cracked with age. In these cases you'll need to replace them. Shut off the water, drain the faucet, and disconnect the risers before removing the mounting nuts and the faucet (*see pages 52–53*).

If removing the faucet completely presents difficulties and if you have a puttied base, loosen the mounting nuts enough so you can raise the faucet up slightly and replace the putty. (To replace a gasket, you'll have to remove the faucet.)

Scrape away any hardened putty from the sink and from the base plate. Then clean both surfaces using a rag soaked in mineral spirits. When the solvent dries, wipe off any sheen left on the surfaces. Then form a rope of plumber's putty (don't use anything else) about ¼-inch thick by rolling it between your hands. Place the rope on the sink where the base plate will go and make sure there are no gaps in the putty. Tighten the faucet back into position and clean away the excess putty that squeezes out.

If you want to replace a gasket but cannot find a duplicate, purchase a piece of neoprene or rubber about ¼-inch thick. Use the old gasket as a template for cutting a new one.

Many plumbers believe that plumber's putty seals better and lasts longer than a plastic or rubber gasket. The putty must seal at all points, so apply more than is needed and scrape away the excess once the faucet is tightened down.

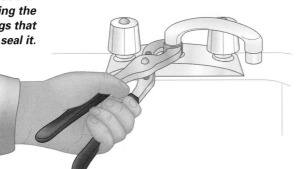

Old putty   Putty knife

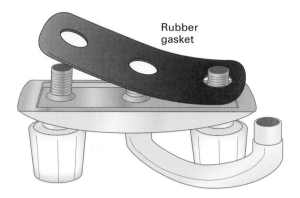

Rubber gasket

Buy a replacement gasket or make one from a sheet of neoprene or rubber.

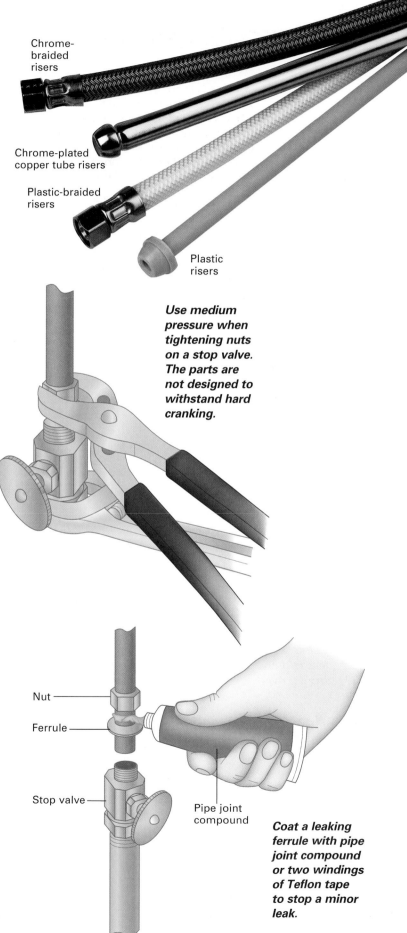

Chrome-braided risers

Chrome-plated copper tube risers

Plastic-braided risers

Plastic risers

Use medium pressure when tightening nuts on a stop valve. The parts are not designed to withstand hard cranking.

Nut

Ferrule

Stop valve

Pipe joint compound

Coat a leaking ferrule with pipe joint compound or two windings of Teflon tape to stop a minor leak.

LEAKY RISERS AND STOP VALVES

If a stop valve or riser (supply line) is leaking, you can tell right away—the leak will be constant. In most cases you can stop the leak by tightening something: the nut attaching the stop valve to the pipe, the stop valve's packing nut (under the handle), the compression nut attaching the stop valve to the riser, or the riser nut at the faucet inlet.

If a copper riser leaks at the stop valve, you also may be able to fix the problem by disassembling and coating the ferrule with pipe joint compound. Tighten the nut firmly before testing.

If a riser is damaged, you have several options for replacing it. Chrome- and plastic-braided risers are flexible and won't kink like copper tubing. They both come complete with nuts, so you can throw away the old compression fillings.

Plastic (not braided) risers are molded with a bulb at the end—the bulb eliminates the need for a ferrule. And, of course you always can use the standard chrome-plated copper risers (some also come with bulb-fittings). The stop valve and the faucet inlet come with ferrules and nuts for attaching flexible copper pipe.

Whatever your choice, make sure you have the right length and thread sizes (both faucets and toilets have two different sizes). Screw the nuts on by hand, then give them a quarter turn or so with pliers. Test and tighten until the leak stops.

REPLACING FAUCETS

Though the inner workings and outer appearance of kitchen and bathroom faucets vary greatly, one-piece units come in only two configurations—center set with 4 inches between the holes and spread set, with holes spaced 8–12 inches apart. If you have an old sink with holes that are differently spaced, you will need to buy a design with separate handles and spout. A bathroom faucet includes a pop-up assembly (*see pages 38-39*). A kitchen faucet may include a sprayer.

REMOVING THE OLD FAUCET

If you have to remove your faucet, clear out the area under the sink. Put towels or a folded drop cloth on the floor to make the working area as comfortable as possible. Have a flashlight, wrenches, a tongue-and-groove pliers, and a basin wrench within easy reach. (A basin wrench is inexpensive and is essential for removing and installing most faucets.) Shut off the stop valve and drain the faucet. If water drips out of the spout even after shutting down the stop valves, or if you have no stop valves, shut off the main valve and open a faucet at a lower point in the house.

DISCONNECT RISERS: Put a small bucket under the stop valve (or pipe-riser connection if there is no stop valve). Loosen the connection with the tongue-and-groove pliers or wrenches, then unscrew by hand. A small amount of water will dribble out. If the nut is hard to reach, dismantling the P trap (*page 16*) may give you more room.

UNSCREW LOCKNUTS AND PULL OUT: For this you will need the basin wrench. Make sure the jaws are set to unscrew; if not, just flip them over. Loosen the nuts with the wrench, then unscrew by hand. Crawl out from under the sink and lift the faucet out. Remove the risers to make it easier to reinstall the new faucet. Scrape and clean the top of the sink.

INSTALL A NEW FAUCET

Inspect the new faucet for thread flaws, marred finishes, and missing parts. If you are replacing the sink at the same time, think through your project—it might be easier to mount the faucet before you install the sink.

MOUNT THE FAUCET BODY: Slip the gasket onto the underside of the faucet, or apply a rope of plumber's putty to the sink top where the faucet base plate will go.

Now for the under-the-counter work. Some faucets are held in place with a nut at each inlet. Others use only one at the spout hole with a single large locknut and washer that fastens to the faucet underbody. Still others use bolts, nuts, and large flat washers (you may have to drill the sink for these).

Position the faucet in the holes and crawl

Use a basin wrench to get at hard-to-reach nuts holding the faucet in place.

Think ahead and decide whether it will be easier to attach the risers to the faucet before or after installing the faucet.

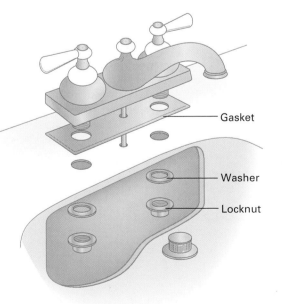

Gasket

Washer

Locknut

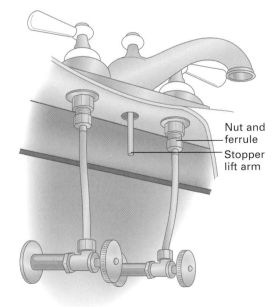

Nut and ferrule

Stopper lift arm

Basin wrench

underneath the sink while a helper holds the faucet in position. Tighten the locknuts partially, then finish tightening with a basin wrench.

CONNECT THE RISERS: If there are no stop valves under the sink, now is the time to install them. Purchase a valve designed to fit the size and type of pipe, as well as your riser. Depending on installation, use a right-angled valve or a straight stop valve. Stop valves can be screwed onto threaded pipe, attached to copper pipe with a compression fitting, or sweated onto copper. Buy the one that is set up to fit both the supply pipe and the riser.

If you use solid chrome-plated risers, cut them with a tube cutter to approximate length, then carefully bend them to shape to prevent crimping. A tubing bender makes this easy (*see page 17*). Make sure the bottom 4–6 inches are plumb so the tubes seat smoothly into the stop valves, and make the final cut. At the bottom of the riser, slip on the nut, then the ferrule. Poke the tube into the stop valve, slide down the ferrule and the nut, and tighten the nut.

Other types of risers are sold in fixed lengths. Use a length that fits between the supply pipe and faucet without kinking. To install a bathroom pop-up assembly, see page 39.

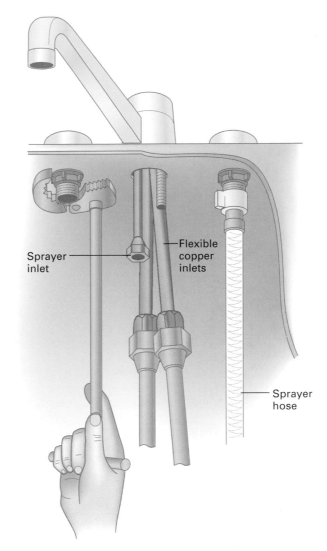

Sprayer inlet

Flexible copper inlets

Sprayer hose

When connecting risers to a unit with flexible copper inlets like these, take special care not to kink the copper inlets; one kink and the faucet will be ruined. Use two wrenches to make the connection.

INSTALLING A ONE-TOUCH

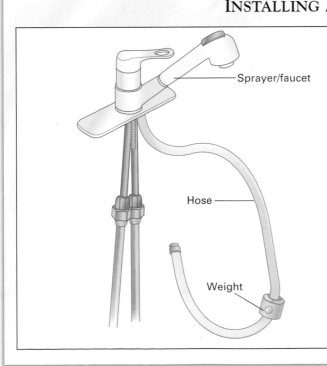

Sprayer/faucet

Hose

Weight

Faucets with spouts that can be pulled out to become sprayers, sometimes called "one-touch" faucets, are increasingly popular. Because they do not need a sprayer diverter valve (*see page 55*), they are more reliable than standard sprayers.

Most of the installation procedures are the same as for a standard kitchen faucet. The unit may attach to the sink via two nuts, one under each handle, or via a single nut and washer in the middle.

The tricky part is ensuring that the spout/sprayer slides freely and easily, and that it returns to its home in the faucet body without fuss. To achieve this, most units use a weight attached to the sprayer hose under the sink. The weight and the hose must be completely free of obstructions. This may mean moving wiring or trap parts out of the way. In addition, once the unit is installed, it is important not to shove cleaning products or rags back into the cabinet, where they may get in the way of the hose.

KITCHEN-SINK DRAINS

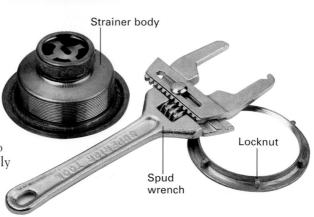

Strainer body

Locknut

Spud wrench

Kitchen sink drains use a removable basket to keep solid things (most of them, anyway) from going down the drain. The strainer fits into a flanged body that is attached to the sink with a retainer and screws (usually older models) or with a locknut.

Many styles of laundry-room sinks use the same installation. If the drain is leaking at the flange, you'll have to remove and reseal it.

REMOVAL

To remove the drain, first remove all the stuff you've stored under the sink. Put it in a box so you won't kick it over.

Disconnect the trap from the tailpiece by unscrewing the slip nuts and pulling the trap pieces apart (*see page 16*).

If you have a large locknut, use a spud wrench to loosen it, and unscrew it by hand. (A pair of channel-type pliers opened all the way may do the trick, but a spud wrench is easier.) If the body of the strainer turns along with the locknut, have a helper hold it in place from above, using a screwdriver and the handles of a pair of pliers (*see below, left*). Lift out the strainer assembly.

If you have a retainer ring, loosen all screws, pry off the metal ring, and remove the unit.

INSTALLATION

Scrape and clean away any old putty and sediment from the drain hole surface, and apply a new rope of plumber's putty around the drain hole. Drop the strainer body into the hole and press down. Have a helper hold the strainer in place using a screwdriver and a pair of pliers while you work from below.

Slip on the new washer, then the friction ring and metal ring (if you have one). Screw on the locknut, and tighten it with a spud wrench, or install the retainer and tighten the locknuts. Plumber's putty will squeeze out around the strainer; lift it away and clean the area with mineral spirits.

Now attach the tailpiece using a new washer, if the old one is worn.

Newer strainers use a simple locknut instead of a retaining ring and three screws.

Remove the body from above by inserting pliers handles and levering with a screwdriver.

Strainer

Body

Washer

Friction ring

Metal ring

Retainer

Coupling nut

Tailpiece

OLD STRAINER

Strainer

Body

Washer

Friction ring

Locknut

Plastic insert

Coupling nut

Tailpiece

NEW STRAINER

KITCHEN SPRAYERS

Sprayers on kitchen sink faucets are notorious troublemakers, plagued by leaks and lack of pressure. On many faucets, the sprayer and its diverter valve are cheaply made, with plastic parts that wear out easily. All models contain tiny orifices that clog easily. Most of the time, a sprayer can be fixed by dismantling and cleaning. Don't be surprised, however, if you have to repeat the repair in less than a year.

TROUBLESHOOTING

If the force of the spray is too low, examine the sprayer hose under the sink. If it is kinked, disconnect it and attempt to straighten it out. If the kink can't be removed, replace the hose.

If the hose isn't kinked, disassemble the sprayer. (You don't have to turn the water off.) If the parts won't unscrew by hand, use pliers lined with a rag to prevent scratching. Keep track of how the pieces go together. Use a toothbrush and vinegar to clean the parts. If they are encrusted or worn, buy a new sprayer.

DIVERTER VALVES

If problems persist even though the hose and sprayer are clear, check the diverter valve.
TWO-HANDLE FAUCET: You don't need to shut the water off. Loosen the ring nut or spout retainer and remove the spout. The diverter valve is usually located in the spout body. Unscrew it and pry it up, or turn a handle on to provide enough water pressure to push it out. Clean the parts, replace any worn rubber or plastic parts, and flush the faucet by turning on the water briefly.

SINGLE-HANDLE FAUCET: On most single-handle faucets, the diverter is located in front of the spout body.

Shut off the water and drain the faucet. Remove the handle and spout, as directed for your faucet type on pages 40–47. Pull the diverter valve out with your fingernail or pry carefully with a knife.

Wash the valve with vinegar and a toothbrush. If an O-ring or washer is worn, take it to your supplier for an exact replacement part or buy a new valve.

Before you reinstall it, gently turn on the water for a few seconds to flush any residue from the faucet body.

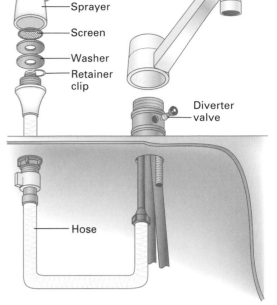

Sprayer diverter valves are usually located somewhere beneath the spout. However, in very old models, the diverter is a part of the aerator at the end of the spout.

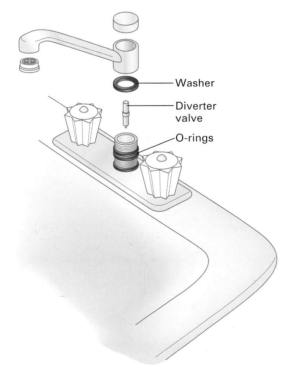

A two-handle faucet usually has its diverter valve positioned vertically in the spout body.

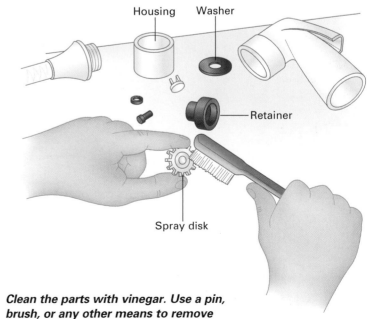

Clean the parts with vinegar. Use a pin, brush, or any other means to remove all particles that can restrict water flow.

INSTALLING KITCHEN SINKS

Replacing a kitchen sink is not a big job as long as the new sink is the same size as the old one. Still, you'll be glad to have help if an assistant is available. If you will be installing a new sink, you will need to provide supply lines, drain and drain line, and disposal, and you'll need to cut a hole in the countertop.

Installing plumbing is easier when you are standing up and have no obstructions. After you've test-fit the sink, attach as much as possible before you install it.

CHOOSING A SINK

Today, nearly all kitchen sinks are rimmed, meaning that they can simply sit on top of a finished countertop surface, with the rim visible. Some sinks made specifically for tiled countertops are designed so that the sink perimeter will be covered by tile (*see opposite page*).

ENAMELED CAST IRON: These sinks are durable, good-looking, and easy to keep clean. They are not easily chipped, but if they are chipped, repair is almost impossible.

ENAMELED STEEL: Lighter-weight steel is less durable and noisier than cast iron.

STAINLESS STEEL: You'll find a variety of finishes and prices. Cheaper models made of steel thinner than 20 gauge may vibrate. Be sure yours has sound-deadening undercoating.

Trap

Disposal

Risers

Faucet

CUTTING THE OPENING

A sink cutout should start 1¾-inches back from the front edge of the countertop. Mark a line at this point parallel to the front edge of the counter.

■ Find and mark the centerline of the sink.

■ Set the sink upside down on the countertop. Center it on the centerline and pull the front edge of the sink about ½ inch forward of the front line. Trace around the sink.

■ Remove the sink and draw the cut line about ½ inch inside the trace line. This ½-inch allowance will be adequate to support the rim and still clear the bowl. Double-check your measurements. Make sure the bowl of the sink will not run into any obstructions below. Cross out or erase the trace line if you marked the hole too big.

■ Drill a ¾-inch hole inside the cut line at each corner and cut with a sabersaw. At the backsplash, saw from below or use a keyhole saw.

■ At the end of the cutout, support the waste piece so it does not fall away and crack the countertop surface.

INSTALLING A CAST-IRON SINK

Set the sink into the hole to make sure it will fit. Take it out, turn the sink upside down, and install as much plumbing as you can—faucet, risers, trap, and garbage disposal. When installing the faucet, position the sink so the faucet holes overhang your work surface. Test-fit the sink again; once you caulk the sink, you will not have much time to finesse the positioning.

Use a caulking gun to apply a bead of silicone caulk to the underside of the sink rim, where it will rest on the countertop. With a helper, ease the sink down into the hole until it is in contact with the counter. Once you are sure the sink is centered, remove the caulk that squeezes out. Use the tip of your finger or dry paper towels to wipe away big globs, then use a rag soaked in mineral spirits to clean the rest. Allow the caulk to set before you hook up the trap and risers below.

INSTALLING A STAINLESS STEEL SINK

A stainless steel sink has a track welded on the underside, running all around the perimeter, which is used to attach the sink to the countertop via special sink clips. The cutout must be precise so that the track fits down inside the cutout rather closely.

Set the sink into the hole to make sure it fits and can be positioned exactly as you want it. Test a couple of sink clips. There are different types of clips, but all have a screw-tightening mechanism and are installed so that one end is caught on the track and the other extends down and over to grab the underside of the counter. When the clip is tightened, the sink is pulled down firmly on the counter. Check to see that you will be able to install the clips all around the sink. You may have to cut the countertop or the inside of the cabinet a bit to make room.

Hook up as much of the plumbing as possible before installing the sink. Place a rope of plumber's putty around the rim or the cutout edge.

Lower the sink into place, taking care that the plumber's putty stays in place. Center the sink and fasten clips about every 6 inches. As you tighten them, putty will squeeze out onto the countertop. If there is an area where no putty squeezed out, it is probably not adequately sealed; when water seeps into this area, it can quickly damage a countertop. From underneath, caulk the unsealed areas with tub and tile caulk so that the edges of the countertop are protected.

With some tiled installations, the sink is positioned first, and the tile is laid to overlap the edge.

A cast-iron sink requires no clips; silicone sealant around the perimeter both seals and provides all the holding power needed.

For sinks set in a tiled backing, install the sink first, then the tile surface.

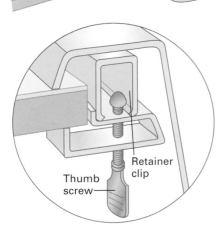

Thumb screw / Retainer clip

Self-rimming sinks that clamp onto the countertop are the easiest to install and the most commonly available.

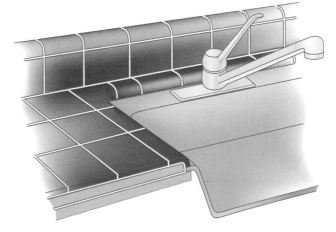

INSTALLING BATHROOM SINKS

Also called lavatories or basins, bathroom sinks are made to install in one of three ways—in a countertop (similar to a kitchen sink—*see pages 56–57*), as a wall-hung, or pedestal units.

These pages explain how to install a wall-hung sink, a pedestal sink, and a vanity. For instructions on assembling traps and hooking up faucets, see pages 16 and 52–53; for running new lines, see pages 86–93.

WALL-HUNG SINK

Wall-hung sinks save space in small bathrooms. The sink may be supported completely by concealed brackets on the wall, or it may use a pair of legs in front for added stability.

A wall-hung sink requires firmly anchored brackets. For extra support, install front legs.

PROVIDING SUPPORT: If you are replacing a wall-hung unit, check to see that the bracket is firmly anchored to the wall and that the bracket style will work with your sink. If not, or if you are installing a wall sink in a new location, you will need to add a strong framing piece to which you will anchor the brackets. Cut a hole in the wall wide enough to give you access to the studs closest to your sink location. Notch the studs and screw a 2×8 in the notches. Attach the bracket by drilling pilot holes and driving ¼-inch lag screws into the brace. Brackets should be level and set at a height somewhat lower than the top of the sink. Hold the sink in place and have a helper mark the bracket position.

Some sinks have holes through which you drive anchor bolts. Drive these very carefully, especially if the sink is porcelain or china. Use cushioning washers to avoid cracking.

PLUMBING AND INSTALLING: Because the trap and supply lines are exposed and there is room to work, plumbing a wall-hung sink is fairly easy. If you will be installing support legs, level the front of the sink while you adjust each for height.

PEDESTAL SINK

Though the pedestal should be tightly fitted between wall, floor, and sink, it is decorative only; the wall bracket does the serious work of supporting the sink.

INSTALL THE BRACKET AND PLUMBING: Provide framing and attach a bracket as you would for a wall-hung sink. To make sure you place the bracket at just the right height, temporarily assemble the basin and the pedestal up against the wall and mark the wall.

Decide whether you want to hide the plumbing. Cramming supply lines and a trap behind a narrow pedestal can be

Brackets

Hot water supply

Cold water supply

Drain

CHOOSING A BATHROOM SINK

If you have the space, a larger sink will give you welcome counter space, and a vanity will add useful storage below. Vitreous china and porcelain are easy to clean and have a finish that will last forever, but they are expensive. Enameled cast iron is also expensive and classy. Fiberglass and plastic materials may advertise themselves as having durable finishes, but they will dull in time. Durable yet inexpensive synthetic marble is an ideal material for a vanity sink.

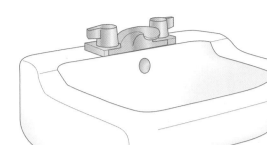

pedestal to the floor with bolts; tighten them carefully.

Once the pedestal and basin are aligned, run a bead of silicone caulk where the pedestal meets the floor. There is no need to caulk the joint where the basin meets the pedestal.

If shoehorning the plumbing behind the pedestal appears to be difficult, consider buying brass or other decorative stop valves and risers and cover only the trap with the pedestal.

Pedestal

a challenge, so either buy a unit with a wide pedestal or get supply lines that look good.

Install the faucet and pop-up assembly on the basin, slip the basin onto the bracket, and hook up the risers and the P-trap. Turn on the water and check for leaks before installing the pedestal.

SLIP IN THE PEDESTAL: Slide the pedestal in and check for plumb. You may have to loosen the nut connecting the tailpiece to the P-trap, so you can lift the basin up slightly. Retighten the tailpiece nut and anchor the

VANITY

This is an easy installation, and since plumbing lines are hidden in the cabinet, you don't have to worry about how they look.

INSTALL THE PLUMBING AND CABINET: If your cabinet has a back, cut holes for the lines and the drain. For a neat installation, shut off water to the house and remove stops so you can precisely mark and drill holes.

Check the cabinet for level and plumb, using shims at the floor or wall if necessary. Drive screws through the cabinet's frame or mounting brackets and into the studs.

INSTALL THE SINK TOP: Hook up the faucet, risers, and pop-up assembly on the sink, and run a bead of silicone caulk on the top edge of the cabinet. Set the sink on the cabinet. Check that it is centered, and see that the backsplash is against the wall. Connect the risers and trap. Cut off the shims with a utility knife and caulk the joint between backsplash, cabinet, and wall.

Installing a new vanity is a quick way to brighten a bathroom and provide storage space. Once the vanity cabinet is installed, cut off the shims using a knife or a hammer and chisel.

Drive a couple of screws into studs.

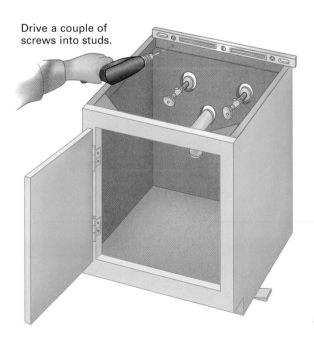

TOILET REPAIRS

A toilet in a typical household might flush thousands of times a year. Given the number of parts inside, it's remarkable that toilets don't need repairs more often than they do. Most of these repairs can be completed easily in a few hours.

HOW IT WORKS

The upper part of a toilet is the **tank**; the lower part, the **bowl**. A spud gasket seals the joint between the tank and bowl; a **wax ring** or a ring made of plumber's putty seals the toilet at the floor.

When the toilet's **flush handle** is flipped, it lifts a **flapper** (or, in old models, a **tank ball**) at the bottom of the tank, allowing stored water to rush down into the bowl. The resulting water pressure is strong enough to push waste through the toilet's **trap** and out to the drain.

A toilet's ball-cock valve, whether controlled by a horizontal float ball or a vertical float cup, allows water to fill the tank. When the flapper opens, gravity sends water into the bowl and down the drainpipe.

When the tank empties, the **float ball** or **float cup** descends, causing the **ball cock**, which is essentially a stop valve, to open and allow water to enter the tank. The water also fills the trap in the bowl through a **refill and overflow tube**. Once the tank is nearly empty, the flapper or tank ball closes down on the **flush valve**, allowing the tank to refill with water. As it fills, the float ball or float cup rises and shuts off the ball-cock valve when the water is at the correct height.

ADJUSTMENTS AND MINOR REPAIRS

Most toilet problems can be fixed by adjusting or replacing inexpensive parts. Use the chart (*opposite*) to help troubleshoot your toilet.

ADJUSTING A FLOAT: If a toilet runs continuously, either the ball-cock valve is not shutting off completely or the flapper is not sealing completely.

Check the water level inside the tank. It should be about ¾ inch below the top of the overflow tube. If it is too high, the valve is not shutting off soon enough and the excess water will spill into the bowl through the overflow tube. Adjust the float ball or cup.

There are two ways to adjust a float ball: Turn the adjustment screw on the brass rod by the ball cock or (and many professional plumbers do this) simply bend the brass rod to lower the float ball. Make sure the float ball can move freely. The lower the float, the sooner the ball-cock valve will shut off.

If you have a float-cup arrangement, a squeezable spring clip will allow you to adjust it up or down. If the valve won't shut off, repair the valve (*see page 63*).

CHAIN AND HANDLE ADJUSTMENTS: To tighten a loose handle, tighten the nut that holds the handle in place and check all the connections for smooth operation.

Sometimes the connecting chain is not properly adjusted. It can get tangled, or it may be too tight, so that the flapper cannot seat. With the flapper closed, there should

Float-cup assembly

Ball-cock valve assembly

Refill tube

Overflow tube

Adjusting spring clip

Float cup

Ball-cock valve

Flush handle

Lift chain

Flush valve

Float ball

Tank

Flapper

Rim openings

Trap

Bowl

Wax ring

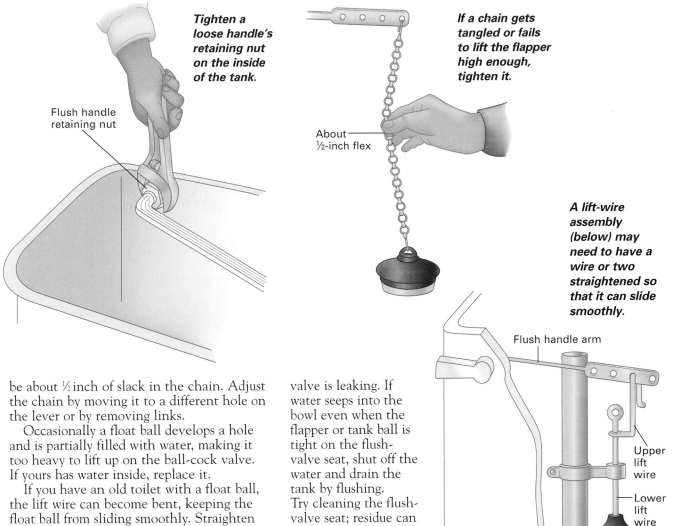

Tighten a loose handle's retaining nut on the inside of the tank.

Flush handle retaining nut

If a chain gets tangled or fails to lift the flapper high enough, tighten it.

About ½-inch flex

A lift-wire assembly (below) may need to have a wire or two straightened so that it can slide smoothly.

Flush handle arm

Upper lift wire

Lower lift wire

be about ½ inch of slack in the chain. Adjust the chain by moving it to a different hole on the lever or by removing links.

Occasionally a float ball develops a hole and is partially filled with water, making it too heavy to lift up on the ball-cock valve. If yours has water inside, replace it.

If you have an old toilet with a float ball, the lift wire can become bent, keeping the float ball from sliding smoothly. Straighten it by hand or with pliers so it glides easily.

FLAPPER OR TANK-BALL REPAIRS:
To test whether water is leaking through the flush valve, put a few drops of food coloring in the tank. If the tinted water shows up in the bowl without flushing the toilet, the flush valve is leaking. If water seeps into the bowl even when the flapper or tank ball is tight on the flush-valve seat, shut off the water and drain the tank by flushing. Try cleaning the flush-valve seat; residue can cause an incomplete seal. Or, the flapper or tank ball may be cracked or worn. Take yours to a supplier for an exact replacement.

TOILET PROBLEMS AND SOLUTIONS

Problem	Solution
Bowl overflows, or flushes incompletely	An auger should clear most obstructions from the toilet or the drain line (*see page 29*). If that doesn't work, try augering the drain line through a cleanout (*see page 28*). If the auger reaches a rigid obstruction, such as a pen or toy, and can't remove it, you may need to remove the toilet to clear the line and restore full function (*page 28*).
Water runs continuously into the tank or bowl	If the water level in the tank is too high, adjust the chain or the float. If the flapper or tank ball is worn, it will allow water to trickle into the bowl; replace it. Otherwise, the ball-cock valve may need to be repaired or replaced.
Water sprays out of the tank	Reattach the refill tube so it squirts into the overflow tube.
Leaky tank	The spud gasket or the gasket for the supply line may have to be tightened or replaced. If the tank is cracked, replace it.
Bowl leaks onto the floor	Usually, the wax ring has lost its seal. Remove the toilet and replace the wax ring (*pages 64–65*). If the bowl is cracked, replace it.

BALL COCK REPAIRS

I f the float is pulling up on the ball cock and the flapper is sealing well, but water continues to run—then you need to repair or replace the ball-cock valve.

Sometimes an old assembly can become belligerent. No matter how many times you adjust the chain or lift rod, you still have to jiggle the handle in order to stop water from running into the bowl. Don't fight it; it just isn't worth the aggravation. The best solution is to replace the old assembly with a newer float-cup unit. The new unit will include a new ball-cock valve.

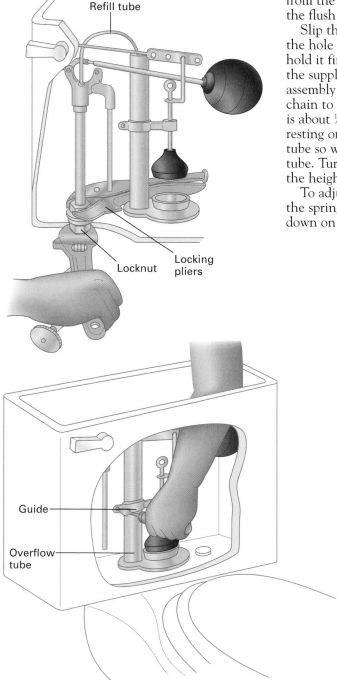

Installing a float-cup assembly replaces most of the mechanical guts—the float ball, the ball-cock valve, and the flapper.

Remove the tank-ball assembly from the overflow tube and unhook it from the flush-handle arm.

Shut off the water to the toilet. Flush twice, then sponge up the water that remains on the bottom of the tank. Place an old dishpan or a bucket under the tank.

Inside the tank and at the bottom, clamp locking pliers onto the nut that holds the old ball-cock assembly in place. On the underside of the tank, use a crescent wrench or locking pliers to loosen the nut where the riser enters. Remove the refill tube from the overflow tube and pull the whole assembly—including the float ball—from the tank.

Remove the flapper or tank-ball assembly from the overflow pipe and unhook it from the flush arm.

Slip the new float-cup assembly through the hole in the tank, and tighten the nuts to hold it firmly and seal off any leaks. Attach the supply lines. Slide the new flapper assembly down the overflow pipe. Bend the chain to the handle lever, and adjust so there is about ½ inch of slack when the flapper is resting on the flush valve. Hook the new refill tube so water will squirt into the overflow tube. Turn the water on, check for leaks and the height of water in the tank.

To adjust the height of a float cup, squeeze the spring clip on the float and push it up or down on the float rod.

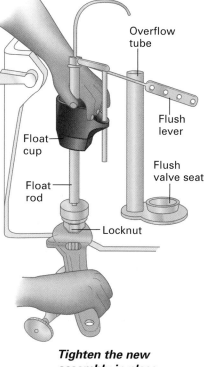

Tighten the new assembly in place.

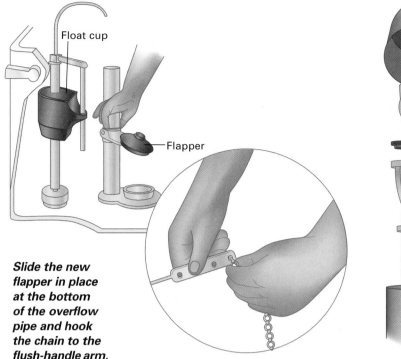

Float cup

Flapper

Slide the new flapper in place at the bottom of the overflow pipe and hook the chain to the flush-handle arm.

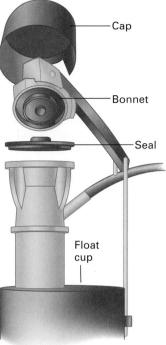

Cap

Bonnet

Seal

Float cup

Float cup and diaphragm valves are simple; replacing a worn rubber part is the most common repair.

REPAIRING BALL-COCK VALVES

Often, only a minor repair is needed for a ball-cock valve—usually a seal or washer needs to be replaced. New ball-cock valves aren't expensive, however, so you might choose to replace a faulty one rather than to repair it.

FLOAT-CUP BALL COCK: Shut off the water and flush the toilet. Pry or pull off the cap. To remove the bonnet, push down on it and turn counterclockwise until it comes free. Clean out any debris. There is a rubber seal located under the bonnet; replace it if it is defective. If the housing or shaft is cracked or worn, replace the whole assembly.

DIAPHRAGM BALL COCK: This has a plastic housing and a metal rod—the float arm—leading to the float. To repair it, shut off the water and flush the tank. Remove the four screws from the top and lift up the bonnet attached to the float arm.

There is a large rubber diaphragm under the bonnet, and a plunger that can be pulled out. Clean away any debris and take cracked or worn rubber parts to a supplier for exact replacements. If the housing is worn, install a new assembly.

PLUNGER-VALVE BALL COCK: This is an old type, but the brass parts can last for a very long time. Shut off the water and flush the toilet. Remove the two thumbscrews and lift

out the float-rod mechanism. Disconnect the refill tube. Pull up on the plunger by hand or use pliers. There will be a seat washer at the bottom, which works much like the washer on a compression-stem faucet (*page 40*). If it is worn, water will trickle through constantly. You also will find washers or packing on the stem; very old units used leather washers. Take the valve to a supplier for replacement parts.

Bonnet

Plunger

Diaphragm

Plunger

Washers

Seat washer

Float-rod mechanism

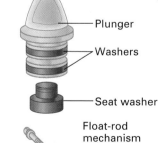

Repair an old ball cock by replacing the seat washer and washers.

REMOVING AND INSTALLING A TOILET

Replacing a toilet may seem like exactly the sort of job you'd want to hire a plumber to do, but you may be pleasantly surprised to find that the job is easier and quicker than you expected. And it is not messy; after a toilet has been flushed, it contains only clean water. The only reasons to replace a toilet are if the one you have is damaged or inefficient or you don't like its style. If you're looking for a new one, consider the following.

Wax ring with plastic sleeve

CHOOSING A TOILET

Older toilets typically use five to seven gallons of water per flush, providing enough water pressure to wash away everything with authority. New regulations in most cities today call for toilets that use only 1.6 gallons. That means reduced flushing power, which can cause a higher incidence of clogged lines. If you have this problem, consider paying extra for a pressure-assisted toilet.

If you have an old toilet and want to save water, there's no need to buy a new toilet; just adjust the float so it shuts off the ball-cock valve at a lower point.

Most toilets have drains centered 12 inches from the back wall. However, some newer space-saving models are centered 10 inches from the wall, so check yours to be sure. Measure to the bowl's hold-down bolts to find the center of the drain.

Some very old toilets have a tank that is bolted to the wall, with a 2-inch chrome elbow that connects the tank to the bowl.

The old bowls in these toilets are often 14 inches from the wall; finding a toilet to match will be difficult; you may have to build the wall out two inches to accommodate a new 12-inch model.

All toilets have a series of small holes under the rim through which water shoots during a flush. Some toilets have an extra "jet" near the bottom of the bowl, which increases flushing power somewhat.

REMOVING A TOILET

When you remove a toilet, take care to remove as much water as possible. Shut off the water at the stop, flush, and sponge up any water that remains in the tank. Scoop out water from the bowl as well.

On the bottom of the tank, loosen the supply nut that holds the ball cock in place. You may have to hold the ball-cock nut

To remove a hold-down bolt that has rusted solid, use a hacksaw to saw down alongside the bolt. Once you saw through the bolt, it will come off easily.

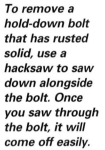

Hanger bolts

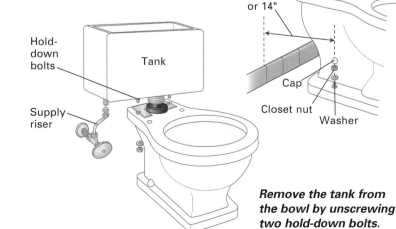

Hold-down bolts

Tank

Supply riser

10", 12", or 14"

Cap

Closet nut

Washer

Bowl

Remove the tank from the bowl by unscrewing two hold-down bolts.

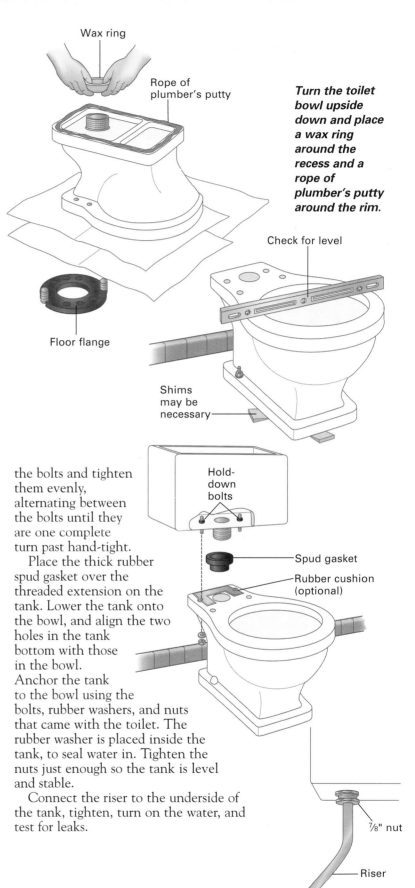

FLANGE EXTENDER

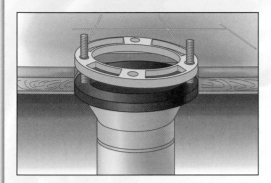

If the floor flange is recessed below the floor surface (perhaps because a new tile surface has been installed), the easiest solution is to use two wax rings; the second ring should have no plastic sleeve, and is placed on top of the first ring while the bowl is upside down. Another way to solve the problem is to buy a flange extender, which raises the flange itself using flexible gaskets and a plastic extender ring.

Turn the toilet bowl upside down and place a wax ring around the recess and a rope of plumber's putty around the rim.

Wax ring

Rope of plumber's putty

Floor flange

Check for level

Shims may be necessary

Hold-down bolts

Spud gasket

Rubber cushion (optional)

⅞" nut

Riser

⅜–½" nut

Stop valve

Unlike a faucet riser, a toilet riser connects to the ball-cock assembly with a ⅞-inch nut and to the stop valve with a ⅜- to ½-inch nut.

inside the tank with locking pliers. Unscrew the closet nuts and washers at the base of the bowl. If they are corroded, they may break off, which is fine. If a nut spins without loosening, cut the bolt with a hacksaw or a metal-cutting blade on a reciprocating saw.

Remove the tank from the bowl by cutting or undoing the bolts that join them. Rock the bowl until the seal at the floor is broken and the toilet comes free. Keep the bowl level as you remove it, so water does not spill out.

Use a putty knife to scrape the old seal off the floor and to clean out the slots for the new closet bolts.

INSTALLING A TOILET

Slip the heads of two new closet bolts into the slots in the closet flange and center them on each side of the flange. Fix them in an upright position, using a dab of plumber's putty.

Turn the new bowl upside down and apply a rope of plumber's putty to the underside rim. Install a wax ring by pressing it onto the recess in the bottom of the toilet. If your wax ring has a plastic sleeve, the sleeve should extend an inch or so into the floor flange when the bowl is installed.

With a helper, lower the bowl carefully, so the bolts slip through the holes. As soon as it contacts the floor, rock it gently to squeeze out the putty. Slip the washers and nuts onto

the bolts and tighten them evenly, alternating between the bolts until they are one complete turn past hand-tight.

Place the thick rubber spud gasket over the threaded extension on the tank. Lower the tank onto the bowl, and align the two holes in the tank bottom with those in the bowl. Anchor the tank to the bowl using the bolts, rubber washers, and nuts that came with the toilet. The rubber washer is placed inside the tank, to seal water in. Tighten the nuts just enough so the tank is level and stable.

Connect the riser to the underside of the tank, tighten, turn on the water, and test for leaks.

Hooking up the plumbing for a washing machine makes a good first project, since supply lines and drainpipes usually are readily accessible, and installation in utility areas doesn't have to be positioned with great precision.

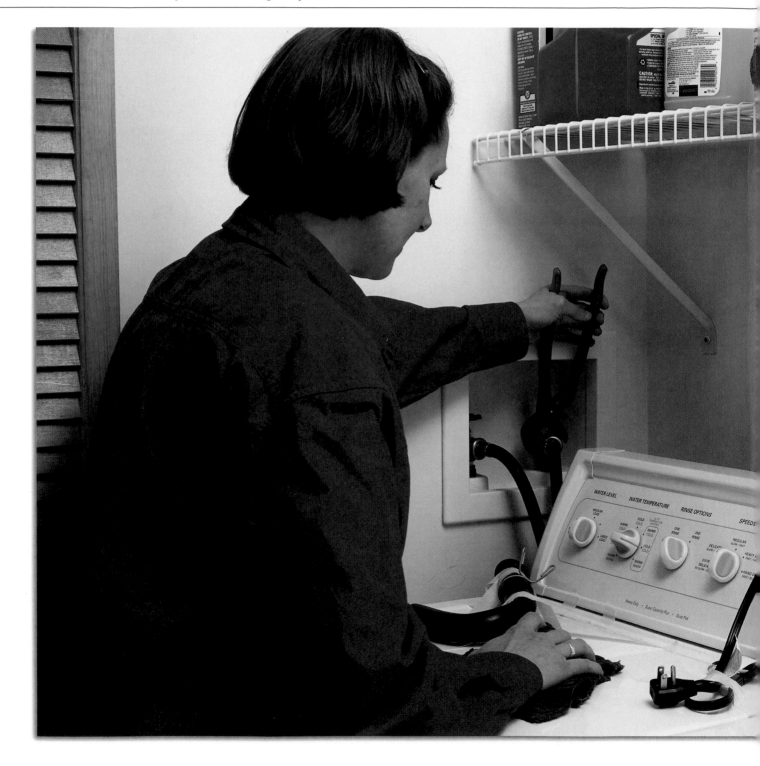

PLUMBING APPLIANCES

The word "appliance" typically refers to a piece of movable equipment that is set or hung in place— as opposed to a "fixture," which is bolted or otherwise fixed in position. An appliance is a machine designed to perform a specific task—usually mechanically—and is hooked up to the plumbing system, and often to the electrical and heating systems as well.

This chapter explains how to hook up the most common household appliances: water heaters, garbage disposals, dishwashers, hot-water dispensers, icemakers, and water filters.

INSTALLING A WASHING MACHINE

A washing machine is easy to install once the supply and drain lines have been run. A laundry supply unit, like the one shown recessed in the wall, keeps all of your controls in easy reach. The most important consideration is that the drain hose be securely attached through a P-trap to a 2-inch standpipe or to a sink front which can be connected to a standard 1½-inch drainpipe by a reducer coupling. A standpipe is a vertical pipe extending down to the trap. It receives the drain hose of the washer so that soapsuds will have room to expand without spilling out the top during the discharge cycle. The standpipe should be 18–30 inches long, and the P-trap must be no higher than 18 inches above the floor.

The drain hose also can empty into a utility sink, or "slop sink." Plastic utility sinks are inexpensive and give you a handy place to clean up after messy projects.

Use hot and cold hose bibbs (outdoor-type faucets) for the shutoffs. Position them behind the machine's control panel at a height of 42 or 48 inches to make them easier to reach.

WATER HEATERS

A water heater is usually tucked out of sight and out of mind; we think about it only when something goes wrong. But a few simple procedures can forestall the day when you have to replace or repair yours. Many repairs are done easily by a homeowner; and, if you are ambitious, you may even want to tackle replacing one. The next seven pages discuss all you need to know.

HOW THE WATER GETS HOT

In both gas and electric water heaters, cold water (usually 50–60° F) enters the top of a vertical tank and is conducted to the bottom through an internal dip tube. Heat is supplied by a gas burner below the tank or by two electric heating elements that extend into the tank, one near the bottom and one near the middle. When the water is hot enough, a thermostat tells the burner or elements to stop heating. Gas water heaters have a flue, which carries heated air and unburned gas through the roof. An electric unit needs no flue.

EFFICIENCY AND HEAT RECOVERY RATE

Most water heaters made today are reasonably energy-efficient. The metal nameplate or yellow energy-rating sticker will tell you how well insulated the unit is, as well as the recovery rate—how quickly it can heat cold water.
INSULATION: An older water heater may not be well insulated, and the resulting lost heat will mean higher energy bills. Feel the outside of your unit while it is heating. If the sides feel very warm (it's normal for the top to feel fairly hot), adding insulation may save you money in the long run. Purchase a water heater insulating jacket that is the right size for your heater.
If you're replacing a water heater with a new unit, look for an R value of 7 or greater.

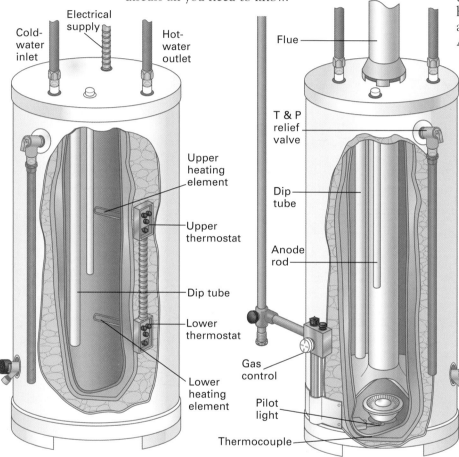

ELECTRIC WATER HEATER

GAS WATER HEATER

Your water heater, whether gas or electric, is essentially an insulated cylinder into which cold water flows and is heated. Electric heaters have no flue and have an electric hookup. If yours is a gas unit, you'll easily spot the flue and the black gas line.

THE BEST TEMPERATURE

Often, the best way to save on water-heater energy costs is to turn the thermostat down so that you need to add very little cold water in order to take a shower that is as hot as you like it. If the water is extremely hot, people usually do not turn the hot water down; they turn the cold water up, so that just as much hot water is used. The only reason to have scalding-hot water is if you have low water pressure; being able to mix in more cold water may make for a more satisfying shower.

RECOVERY RATE: Recovery—the time required to heat water—depends on how efficiently heat is applied to the tank, not how well insulated it is. So a well-insulated unit still may take a long time to get the water hot after it has been depleted.

The information plate on the heater states how many gallons it will heat in one hour, as well as how high the temperature will be raised. If you often run out of hot water, the usual solution is to buy a larger tank rather than one with a higher peak temperature.

MAINTENANCE

DRAIN THE TANK: The primary reason water heaters die prematurely is sediment buildup in the tank. Regular flushing of a water heater will typically double its life.

Twice a year, or more often if your water is particularly sediment-laden, turn off the shutoff valve at the top of the water heater. Place a bucket under the drain valve, or hook up a garden hose and run it to a floor drain. Open the drain valve and let it run until the water runs completely clear. Close the drain valve and turn on the water. Not all drain valves are made to stand frequent use; in buying extra time for your water heater, you may have to replace the drain valve.

RELIEF VALVE: At or near the top, you will find a temperature-and-pressure relief valve. This safety device will open if the water temperature or pressure gets too great. The chances of this happening are slim, but the tank could burst if the valve did not do its job. If you have an old unit without a relief valve, have one installed.

Test the relief valve a couple times a year:

Pull on the handle briefly. If water spurts out, it's working. If it doesn't, replace the valve. Shut off the water coming into the tank, and turn off the gas or the breaker supplying electric power. Drain some of the water, so the water level will be below the relief valve. Release any pressure slowly by opening the valve, let the water cool or drain it completely. Use a wrench or pliers to unscrew the drainpipe attached to the valve (if any) and the valve itself. Buy an exact replacement. Wrap Teflon tape around the joints, and screw the new valve tight.

ANODE TUBE: Many water heaters have an anode tube, which works sort of like flypaper to collect sediment. Unscrew it from the top of the heater and pull it out. If it is heavily encrusted, replace it. Newer "self-cleaning" water heaters do not have anode tubes.

Flushing your water heater twice a year can double its life. To flush the unit, turn off the cold-water valve and open the drain valve until the water runs clear.

Drain valve

Twice a year, test the relief valve by pulling the handle out briefly. If no water spurts out, replace the valve.

Relief valve

WATER HEATER PROBLEMS AND REPAIRS

Problem	Solution (see pages 70–73 for instructions.)
No hot water—gas unit	Check that the gas and the control knob are on. If the pilot light is not burning, relight. If the pilot won't stay lit, replace the thermocouple. If the pilot light is lit and there is still no hot water, clean the burner and the burner ports.
No hot water—electric unit	Check the electrical service panel and reset a tripped breaker or replace a blown fuse. If the unit continues to blow fuses or trip the breaker, call in an electrician.
Water not hot enough	Check the thermostat. Drain the tank if you have not done so recently. On an electric unit, the upper element or thermostat may have burned out; replace it.
Tank makes noise	Drain the tank; sediment can cause noise.
Hot water runs out quickly	First try draining the tank. If water must travel a long way to get to the fixtures, insulating the pipes will help. On an electric unit, the lower heating element may need to be replaced. If gas burner flames look orange or incomplete, clean the burner unit or call the gas company. If the tank is not big enough for your family, buy a larger one.
Leaks	If the relief valve leaks, replace it. If the leak is from the tank base, replace the water heater.

GAS WATER HEATER REPAIRS

I f a gas unit suddenly stops heating, the pilot light has probably gone out. Clear the area so you can work comfortably, and remove the access panels—there will be two—located under the thermostat control. Always replace the access panels when you are done; otherwise, the pilot light can be easily blown out.

BURNER AND THERMOCOUPLE REPAIRS

Keep the area around the burner fairly free of dust. Simply vacuum the area occasionally, so particles don't impede the gas flow.

LIGHTING A PILOT: Instructions specific to the unit will be printed on its side, but this is the general procedure: Turn the indicator knob to OFF for a minute or two, to make sure no excess gas is hanging around when you strike a match. Turn the knob to PILOT, the only position that allows you to push the reset button down all the way. Light a long fireplace match or a thin piece of wood (don't use rolled-up paper), depress the button, and hold it down while you light the pilot.

To relight a pilot, open the access panel near the base of the unit where gas and thermocouple lines enter.

Fireplace match

Pilot-light access panel

CARBON MONOXIDE

A colorless and odorless gas, carbon monoxide (CO) is one of the most common forms of indoor pollution. Its effects are usually subtle: Headaches, fatigue, and nausea are some symptoms.

Faulty water-heater flues and inefficiently burning boilers are two of the most common sources. In addition to checking your flue (*page 71*), install a CO detector in a room directly above or near your boiler and water heater. If CO is detected, your gas company will come out and be able to tell you where any leaks are coming from. Some gas companies check for CO free of charge.

After about 45 seconds, release the reset button; the pilot should stay on. Turn the indicator knob to ON, and the burners will fire up with a "whump."

REPLACING A THERMOCOUPLE: If the pilot goes out every time you release the reset button, you probably need to replace the thermocouple, a safety device that generates an electrical current when exposed to heat. It is a long, thin tube with a sensing bulb at the end. The bulb is clamped in position so that the pilot flame heats it and the thermocouple current keeps the valve open. If the pilot light goes out or the thermocouple wears out, it won't generate current and the flow of gas is shut off.

Detach a defective thermocouple from the control box and unclip it from next to the pilot light.

Thermocouple lead

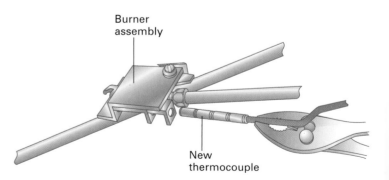

Burner assembly

New thermocouple

Install a new thermocouple by pushing it into the clip in the burner assembly.

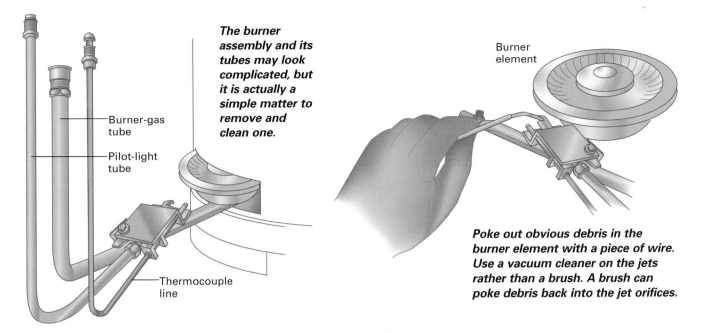

Burner-gas tube

Pilot-light tube

Thermocouple line

The burner assembly and its tubes may look complicated, but it is actually a simple matter to remove and clean one.

Burner element

Poke out obvious debris in the burner element with a piece of wire. Use a vacuum cleaner on the jets rather than a brush. A brush can poke debris back into the jet orifices.

To replace a thermocouple, either remove the whole burner assembly, *above,* or reach in and unhook the thermocouple bulb. Make a careful mental note of where the new bulb should go. Remove the line at the valve by unscrewing a compression nut. Replace it with a new thermocouple of the same length. Because of the expansion and contraction of the tube, a sensing bulb that is not firmly held in place may come loose and malfunction.

CLEANING A BURNER: If the burner flames are yellowish instead of steady blue, or if the burner gives off smoke, remove and clean the burner and its tubes. (You also may want to do this if you've had to remove the burner to disconnect a hard-to-reach thermocouple.)

Shut off the gas. There are three tubes connected at the thermostat: the pilot-light tube, the burner-gas tube, and the thermocouple. Unscrew the nuts for them all, pull the tubes down from the thermostat gently, and pull the entire burner assembly out of the heater.

Unscrew the burner element from the tube. Use a thin piece of wire to ream out the orifices where the tube enters the burner and at the end of the pilot-light tube. Vacuum out dust and debris from the burner jets. Replace and reconnect the burner assembly and test. If the flames are still yellow or give off smoke, call your gas company for an inspection.

TESTING AND MAINTAINING A FLUE

A flue that is not properly configured, that is clogged, or that has loose joints can leak carbon monoxide and other harmful fumes into your home. First test the draw: Light a

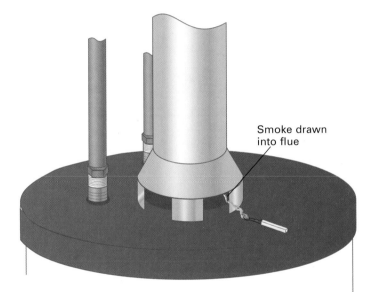

Smoke drawn into flue

match or a small piece of paper, blow it out, and place it near the the bottom of the flue. If the smoke is not sucked out with authority, the flue may need cleaning. Also inspect the joints for leaks: Hold a lit match or candle near each joint; if the flame is sucked toward the joint, it needs to be tightened.

To clean a flue, shut off the gas to the water heater. Disassemble the parts by removing screws. Remove only a few pieces at a time and keep track of how they fit together. Use a rag and a stick, or a special brush made for cleaning flue pipe, to remove most of the gunk clinging to the inside of the pipes. Reassemble with screws.

To tighten joints, drill pilot holes and drive sheet-metal screws at the loose spots. Do not rely on duct tape.

Test your flue by striking a match and checking that the smoke runs up inside.

ELECTRIC WATER HEATER REPAIRS

When an electric water heater produces little or no heat, start by looking at the simple causes:
■ Make sure the fuse is not blown or that the circuit breaker is not tripped.
■ Check the settings on thermostats.
■ Drain sediment from the tank (*see page* 69). If those steps do not solve your problem, a thermostat or heating element is most likely the culprit.

Even after you've turned off the power, use a neon tester or voltmeter to double-check that no power is present. Touch the probes of the tester to the two upper terminal screws of the thermostat.

Change the temperature setting by adjusting the thermostat with a standard screwdriver.

CAUTION

Exercise great caution when working on an electric water heater. Most household receptacles and appliances use 120 volts, enough to give you quite a jolt; water heaters use 240 volts, enough to do serious harm or even kill you. Always turn power off at the service panel by shutting off the circuit breaker or pulling the fuse.

DIAGNOSING PROBLEMS

It's easy to tell which element or thermostat needs to be replaced in an electric heater.
■ If your water suddenly does not get hot enough, the upper heating element or upper thermostat (those nearer the heater's water outlet) should be replaced.
■ If water is hot but there is less hot water than previously, the lower heating element or lower thermostat (those farther from the outlet) is defective.

If water gets too hot, even though the thermostats are adjusted properly, the high-temperature cutoff may be defective. This is located next to the upper thermostat. Often the thermostat and cutoff are linked together as one unit, but on some models you can replace one without replacing the other. You may want to buy both, try them one at a time, and return the one you don't need.

Many plumbers automatically replace the thermostat whenever they replace a heating element, because when one goes, the other

REPLACING THE THERMOSTAT

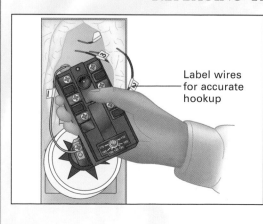

Label wires for accurate hookup

Shut off power at the service panel and test for the presence of power at the thermostat. Disconnect all four wires and label them so you know where they go. Pull the thermostat out by hand or use a screwdriver to gently pry it out. Purchase a correct replacement. Snap the new thermostat in and reattach the wires. Set the thermostat to the desired temperature (use a screwdriver). You may need to push the reset button as well. Replace the cover and restore electrical power.

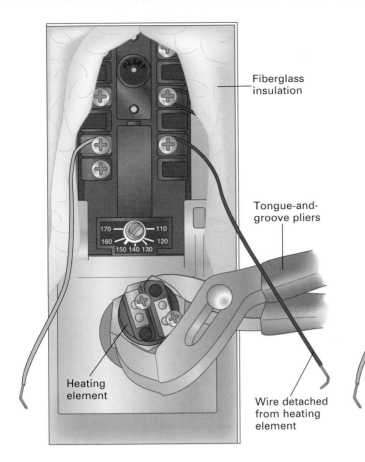

Fiberglass insulation

Tongue-and-groove pliers

Heating element

Wire detached from heating element

Once you make sure the power is off, replacing an element or a thermostat is a safe, simple job. Take the old element with you when buying the replacement.

may soon fail as well. If you have more time than money, however, replace one or the other. Usually it is the heating element rather than the thermostat that fails.

REMOVE AND REPLACE AN ELEMENT

Shut off the power. Remove the cover plate for the thermostat or heating element that seems to be acting up and test for power. Drain the water heater so the water is below the level of the thermostat (*see page 68*). You may need to push some fiberglass insulation and a protective plastic flap out of the way.

Disconnect the two wires that lead to the element and label them so you know where each one goes. Pull off the round element cover. Use tongue-and-groove pliers to unscrew the element and pull it out.

Take the heating element to a supplier for an exact replacement. Smear a bit of pipe joint compound on both sides of the new element's gasket, slide it in, and screw it in with the pliers. Reconnect the wires, the round cover, and the cover plate. Restore power and test; give the water heater an hour or so to heat the water.

WATER-HEATER TIMER

A 24-hour-dial time switch lets you turn off your electric water heater when hot water isn't needed, cutting the unit's use of power by as much as 25 percent. Simply install a time switch rated for the amps of your heater and wire it into the electric line feeding the heater. Program the timer to match your schedule. For example, you could set it to turn on the heater an hour before you need it (5 a.m. for a 6 a.m. wake-up) and turn it off half an hour before you leave. Program a similar pattern for the afternoon, so water is hot from your arrival home until bedtime.

REPLACING A WATER HEATER

Gas water heaters typically last 10–15 years; electric units can last twice as long. Replacing either type is not as expensive or as difficult as you may think. It requires only two water connections and either an electric or a gas connection.

Before you remove the old unit, plan your hookups. Though flexible lines are available for both gas and water lines, pros usually prefer to hard-pipe everything; flexible water lines are expensive and may not be permitted by your local code.

To remove a water heater, disconnect water pipes and gas supply pipe (or electric wire) and remove the flue pipe from a gas unit.

Flue

Hot-water outlet pipe

Cold-water inlet pipe

Gas supply

REMOVAL

Getting rid of the old heater can be messy and strenuous. Make the job easier by clearing the area around the tank so you'll have room to work.

DRAIN: Shut off the water supply line leading to the tank. Drain the tank completely, using a garden hose leading to a floor drain. (To speed the draining, open an upstairs hot-water faucet.)

DISCONNECT: While the tank is draining, shut off the gas or electricity; on a gas unit, it may take a minute or two for the pilot light to go out. Then disconnect the gas line. Use two pipe wrenches to open the union (*see page 25*). Dismantle enough of the flue so you can easily move the water heater out.

On an electric unit, shut off the water-heater circuit at the service panel and test for power (*see page 72*). Remove the electrical cover

If the water pipes are sweated copper, you will have to cut them.

Tube cutter

plate on or near the top of the tank and disconnect the wires. Mark the wires so you'll know how to reattach them. Loosen the cable setscrew and pull the cable out.

Disconnect the water lines—opening a union if you have galvanized pipe, unscrewing the nuts on flexible lines, or cutting copper pipe with a tubing cutter or hacksaw.

CART THE TANK AWAY: A tank full of sediment can be heavy, so have a helper on hand and use a cart, if possible. Short lengths of pipe left on the heater make useful handles.

INSTALLATION

Choose a new water heater with hookups similar to your old one to save yourself the trouble of installing new piping. If there is no floor drain nearby, set the water heater in a special pan to collect water in case it leaks.

FLUE CONNECTIONS (GAS ONLY): Position your gas unit with an eye to reconnecting the flue. Flues work best when they make as few turns as possible. Water and gas are not affected by turns. Position the heater so your flue has as straight a run as possible. If any of the flue pipes or fittings are severely rusted, replace them. Buy an adjustable 90-degree elbow, which can be rotated to achieve just about any bend. Dry-fit and hang the flue pipe without driving any new screws at the flue joints. Always install so male ends are pointing away from the water heater.

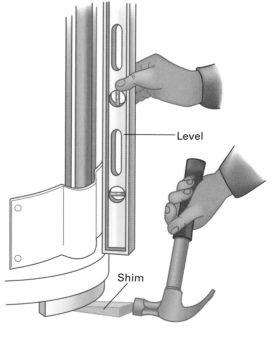

Level

Shim

Level a water heater by tapping wood shims under the legs.

WATER CONNECTIONS: Rotate the tank to simplify water connections as much as possible, but make sure the control box and pilot can be reached easily. Use a level to check the tank for plumb in two directions, and shim if necessary.

Your old water heater may have special nipples on hot- and cold-water inlets. These were designed to conserve energy by preventing the slow migration of cold water into the heater and the upward movement of hot water out of the heater. Remove these, as they can plug up and may inhibit needed pressure relief on the tank.

Check with your water department to see if your main supply has a backflow inhibitor. If it doesn't, you may need to install an expansion tank on the cold-water inlet to keep water from backing into the line due to the expansion of hot water in the tank.

Reattach or install new supply lines and valves. If you are not using flexible lines, install a union in each line so the heater can be removed easily.

RELIEF VALVE: If your unit does not come with one, buy a temperature- and pressure-relief valve (*see page 69*) with the same pressure rating as the water heater. Wrap its threads with Teflon tape and screw it in. You may want to connect an outlet pipe to it as well.

GAS AND FINAL FLUE CONNECTIONS: A flexible gas line may be the easiest to install, but it can develop a leak if it gets bumped hard. Many areas require that the gas line be all black steel pipe on a permanent fixture like a water heater.

Following the directions on pages 24–25, run threaded pipe in the configuration shown at right. The drip leg collects moisture,

ensuring a steady flame. Use pipe joint compound or special gas-pipe Teflon tape, not regular Teflon tape, at all the joints. Finish by hooking up a union.

Drill pilot holes and drive screws to attach the flue sections together.

Turn on the gas and check for leaks by soaking each joint with soapy water. Be sure no bubbles are coming from the joints. Light the pilot (*see page 70*) and adjust the temperature.

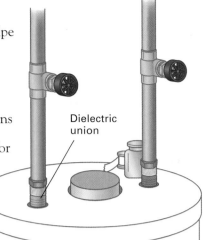

Dielectric union

Some localities allow flexible gas lines for water heaters, but hard pipe provides greater resistance to accidental bumps. Use a dielectric union to make the transition from the copper supply pipe to a small steel nipple emerging from the water heater.

Gas shutoff valve

Union

Drip leg

Thermostat and burner shutoff valve

ELECTRIC WATER HEATER

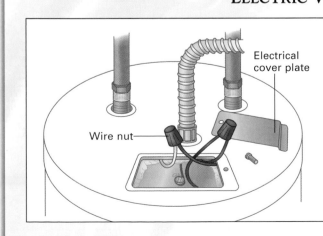

Electrical cover plate

Wire nut

Make water connections for an electric water heater in the same way as for a gas unit.
- With the power shut off, remove the electrical cover plate located at or near the top of the water heater.
- Push the cable through the plate's cable clamp, so that all the unsheathed wires will be inside the tank, and tighten the cable in place.
- Connect the wires in the same way as they were for the old unit, using wire nuts. Push the wires into place and replace the cover plate.
- Adjust the thermostat to the temperature you want and press the reset button.
- Restore power.

GARBAGE DISPOSALS

A new garbage disposal is not difficult to install if you already have a switched receptacle under the sink to plug it into. If you don't have one, then wiring and installing the receptacle will be the greater part of the job.

If you're replacing a disposal, you will save work by buying one with a drain in the same position as the old one. Upgrading to a heavier-duty model may require you to change the drainpipe under the sink.

If you are installing a new sink at the same time as the disposal, hook up the disposal before putting in the sink (*see page 56*).

PROVIDING A SWITCHED RECEPTACLE

The most common type of disposal plugs into an electrical receptacle located below the sink and controlled by a switch positioned conveniently nearby. The best place for the switch is on the wall a foot or so away from the sink; a switch placed on the base cabinet can be accidentally turned on and is an enticement to kids.

If there is no power under the sink, or if the only receptacle is not switched, consult a wiring book or hire an electrician. A receptacle can be "split," so that one of its plugs is hot all the time and the other is controlled by a switch.

Dishwasher drain knockout

You can "hard-wire" the disposal into the junction box with flexible cable instead of plugging it in with a cord. This is usually not necessary; as long as the cord is out of the way, chances of it getting pulled out are slim.

If you have a receptacle that is not switched and do not want to go to the trouble of wiring a switch, purchase a self-switching disposal. It will turn on when food is pushed down into it.

INSTALLING A DISPOSAL

Remove the existing P-trap and the basket strainer (*pages 16 and 52*). Clean out old plumber's putty from around the sink opening.
DISHWASHER DRAIN KNOCKOUT: If you have an electric dishwasher, use needle-nose pliers or a hammer and screwdriver to remove the knockout plug in the disposal's dishwasher drain connection.
MOUNTING ASSEMBLY: The mounting assembly takes the place of a sink drain. Disassemble all the pieces if it came preassembled. Place a rope of plumber's putty around the sink hole and press the flange into it. From below, slip on the rubber gasket and the three-screwed mounting ring. While a helper holds the flange base from above, push the snap ring onto the flange until it snaps into place. Tighten the three screws to force the lower mounting ring down and the upper ring up. This will pull the flange down tight to the sink, squeezing out excess putty. Don't tighten the screws completely yet.
ATTACH THE WIRES AND DRAIN ELBOW: Before you attach the disposal to the mounting assembly, hook up the electrical cord or cable. Remove the cover plate on the bottom to reveal the wires. Strip the wire ends of an appliance cord and connect the wires to the cord with wire nuts. Then clamp the cord tight and reinstall the cover plate.

Drain elbow

P-trap

For a single-bowl installation, connect straight into a P-trap. On a two-bowl sink, purchase an installation kit with the tubular pieces you need to connect both the disposal and the other sink to a P-trap.

Directional waste tee

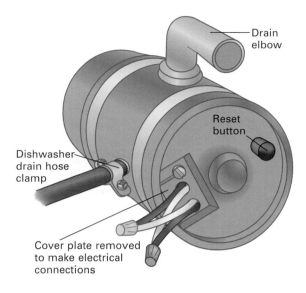

Drain elbow

Reset button

Dishwasher drain hose clamp

Cover plate removed to make electrical connections

If your drainpipe installation requires the drain elbow, attach it to the disposal using the two bolts and a rubber gasket provided with the unit.

INSTALL THE DISPOSAL: This can be difficult if the disposal is heavy and you are working in cramped quarters. Lift the disposal straight up and insert it into the mounting assembly so it is centered. Twist the entire disposal until it is tight. Once the disposal is attached, rotate it to the best position for installing the drain lines and tighten the screws completely.

HOOK UP THE TRAP AND DISHWASHER: There are various ways to configure the disposal drain connection to the drainpipe in the wall; choose the one that suits your situation. If there is only one sink bowl, connect the drain elbow directly to the P-trap. If there are two bowls, install a crossover connection (*see opposite*). Some plumbers prefer to install a separate trap for the disposal.

Kits are available with all the parts you need. If you are reusing your tubular pipes, replace all the rubber gaskets and plastic washers.

For the dishwasher drain, install a length of ⅞-inch hose running either to the dishwasher or to an air gap on top of the sink (*see page 78*). Make sure the hose has no kinks. Secure each hose end with a hose clamp.

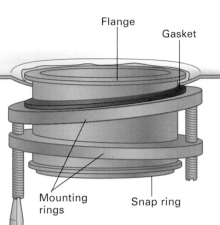

Flange

Gasket

Mounting rings

Snap ring

To install the mounting assembly, first slip on the mounting rings and snap ring, then tighten the adjusting screws.

MAINTAINING YOUR GARBAGE DISPOSAL

Your disposal will come with a tool for freeing the grinder when it gets stuck. It will be either an allen wrench that fits into the hole at the bottom of the disposal or a fork-like tool that you insert from above. Keep this tool handy, because you will eventually need it. Work either tool until the grinder moves freely, then reach in and remove any obstructions. If you don't have the tool, use a broom handle to rotate the grinder from above.

If a disposal overheats, it automatically shuts off to prevent motor damage. A reset button on the bottom pops out. If this happens, turn the disposal switch off. Wait 10 minutes. Push the reset button in hard and the disposal should work again.

Avoid overusing a disposal. It grinds food into a mush, which can clog drains.

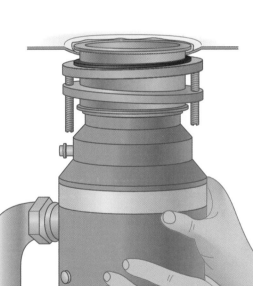

Slip the disposal into the mounting assembly and rotate until it is tight. You can now turn the disposal so the plumbing connections are facing in the most convenient direction.

INSTALLING A DISHWASHER

Though dishwashers vary greatly in style and features, all require three hookups—hot-water supply, drain, and electrical. Replacing a dishwasher is usually an easy job. A new installation will require that you will make an opening that is the right size and run the three lines.

REMOVING AN OLD DISHWASHER

Always turn off electrical power before working on a dishwasher. Damp conditions, exposed electrical connections, and metal tools all can create dangerous situations. Also shut off water to the unit; there may be a stop valve under the sink.

Remove the access panel at the floor; usually it is held by two screws. Have a few towels or sponges within reach to mop up water that will spill. Disconnect the drain hose, the water supply, and the electrical cable.

Look for screws connecting the dishwasher to the underside of the countertop. Remove them and carefully pull out the dishwasher. If it gets stuck, check underneath for obstructing plumbing or electrical lines.

The opening for a standard-size dishwasher must be 24 inches wide and square. Position water supply, drain, and electrical lines so they will not be in the way when you slide the dishwasher in.

Air gap

Dishwasher shutoff valve

Drain hose

Electrical cable

Water supply

24"

PREPARE FOR A NEW INSTALLATION

Most dishwashers are designed to fit snugly in a 24-inch-wide space under a countertop. Your job will be greatly simplified if you can replace a 24-inch base cabinet with a dishwasher. The opening must be a full 24 inches and square at the corners. Drill holes for all three lines as shown in the illustration (*below*).

ELECTRICAL LINE: A dishwasher should have its own electrical circuit, and installing one cable is a somewhat complicated wiring task: Hire an electrician if necessary. A new cable should be long enough to reach the front of the dishwasher and not get in the way when you slide the dishwasher in.

DRAIN LINE: A drain hose may come attached to the dishwasher; if not, buy a dishwasher drain hose.

If you have a garbage disposal, remove the knockout plug in its connection for the dishwasher drain. If not, replace the existing tailpiece on the sink with a dishwasher tailpiece, which has a right-angled inlet for the dishwasher hose. Connect the hose to either of these using a hose clamp.

Some local codes require that the drain hose be connected to a fitting called an air gap. Install the air gap into a knockout hole in the sink, or drill a hole in the countertop. Attach a ⅞-inch hose between the drain and the air gap, and a ⅝-inch hose from the air gap to the dishwasher opening. Some codes may let you omit the air gap if you loop the hose so that at one point it is raised almost as high as the countertop.

If your dishwasher allows front-panel access to the drain outlet, hook up the drain hose after the machine is pushed into its pocket. Otherwise, install the drain line before you move the machine.

WATER SUPPLY: Install a tee in the hot-water supply line. (*See pages 18–19 for working with copper and pages 24–25 for galvanized steel pipe.*) Add a nipple

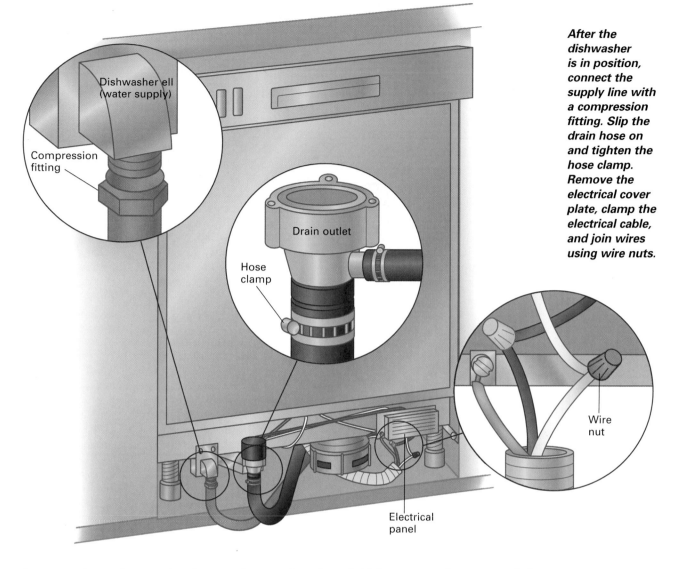

Dishwasher ell
(water supply)

Compression
fitting

Drain outlet

Hose
clamp

Wire
nut

Electrical
panel

*After the
dishwasher
is in position,
connect the
supply line with
a compression
fitting. Slip the
drain hose on
and tighten the
hose clamp.
Remove the
electrical cover
plate, clamp the
electrical cable,
and join wires
using wire nuts.*

and a stop valve with an outlet that matches the size of your dishwasher supply hose—either ⅜ or ½ inch. Run copper tubing from the valve into the dishwasher enclosure.

Gently shape and curve the tubing to run it from the stop valve below the sink to where the front of the dishwasher will be. Slide on compression nuts and ferrules and connect the line to the stop valve.

INSTALL A DISHWASHER

Remove the access panel on the new unit and take note of where each connection will be made. Read the manufacturer's instructions to double-check. Arrange the three lines in the opening so that they will be near their connection points. The copper supply tubing should be positioned accurately, because bending it too much after the dishwasher is in place could easily lead to a kink.

DISHWASHER ELL: If the dishwasher is not equipped to receive the supply tubing with a compression fitting, install a special brass fitting called a dishwasher ell. Wrap its

threads with Teflon tape and screw it tightly into the water-supply inlet on the dishwasher.

MAKE THE CONNECTIONS: Remove all packing and slide the dishwasher into the opening, taking care not to move plumbing or electrical lines.

Hook up the supply line using a compression nut. Slip a hose clamp onto the drain hose, push the hose onto the drain fitting, and secure it with the hose clamp. Join wires with wire nuts, and clamp the cable's sheathing securely.

ALIGN, ANCHOR, AND TEST: Turn the leveling screws (the threaded feet) at the bottom of the dishwasher so that it sits firmly and level. To attach the top of the dishwasher to the underside of the countertop, carefully drill pilot holes (you don't want to poke all the way through the top) and drive screws through the mounting tabs.

Open the stop valve and restore electrical power. Give the dishwasher a thorough test: Run it for a complete cycle, periodically peering underneath with a flashlight to make sure there are no leaks.

HOT-WATER DISPENSERS

Mount the faucet into the sink deck by tightening the mounting nut. Install the mounting bracket and install the heater. Then connect the copper lines and plastic tube.

As long as you have an extra hole on your sink's deck and an electrical receptacle below the sink, this simple installation will allow you to have hot water (200° F) for coffee or soup on demand. If your extra sink hole is occupied by a sprayer, consider installing a one-touch faucet (*see page 53*), thereby freeing up a hole for the hot-water dispenser and giving you a sprayer that is probably more reliable.

PROVIDE A RECEPTACLE: Most codes call for a GFCI (Ground Fault Circuit Interrupter) receptacle under the sink. The same receptacle can be used for the garbage disposal, as long as it is "split" so that the disposal's plug is controlled by a switch and the dispenser's plug is always hot.

CUT A MOUNTING HOLE: To cut a new hole in a stainless steel sink, use a metal-cutting hole saw and drill slowly. Or, put the hole in the countertop, right next to the sink. The dispenser will need to be within two feet of the tank.

PROVIDE THE WATER SUPPLY: The easiest way to supply water is to tap into a hot-water pipe below the sink with a saddle tee valve (see the next page for instructions). If local codes forbid saddle tees, install a tee, a nipple, and a shutoff valve. You'll need an adapter fitting in order to fit the dispenser's supply line into the shutoff valve. Run water through the saddle tee or shutoff valve for a few seconds to clear out any sediment.

INSTALL THE FAUCET: You may need to uncoil the three copper tubes coming out from the base of the faucet. (Be careful to avoid kinking them.) Slip the rubber gasket onto the faucet's threads and insert the threads into the sink hole. While a helper holds the faucet, go beneath and anchor it using a washer and the mounting nut. Tighten with a basin wrench (*see page 52*) or screwdriver, depending on the model. Connect the copper supply line from the saddle tee or stop valve to the faucet.

MOUNT THE TANK: Fasten the tank's mounting bracket under the sink where it will not get bumped. It can either be on the wall or on the side of the cabinet. Slip the tank onto the bracket.

HOOK UP THE PLUMBING: There are two more copper lines to connect, one for cold water and one for hot water. Bend the tubes carefully to avoid kinks and install with the compression nut and ferrule provided. Slip the plastic vent tube in place and tighten it with a hose clamp.

TEST: Turn on the stop or saddle tee valve and check for leaks. Turn on the dispenser knob and hold it open for a minute or so, until water starts coming out. Check for leaks again. Plug the cord for the dispenser into an electrical receptacle. Follow the dispenser manufacturer's instructions for breaking in the system.

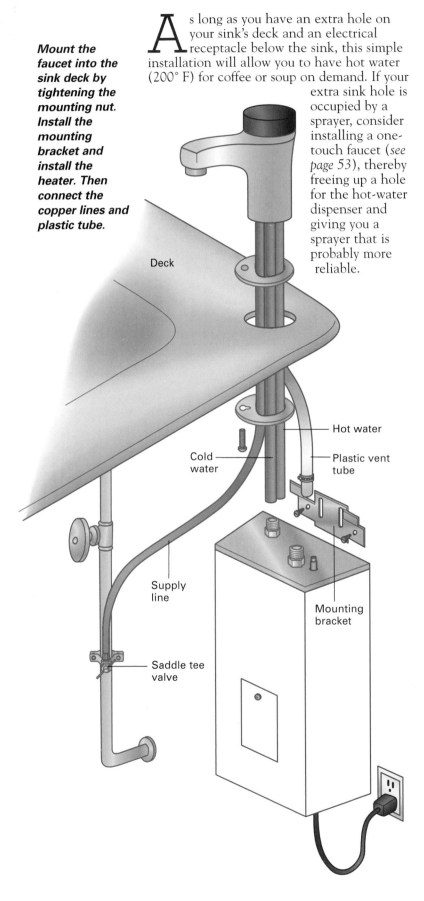

Deck

Hot water

Cold water

Plastic vent tube

Supply line

Mounting bracket

Saddle tee valve

ICEMAKERS

Supplying cold water to a refrigerator icemaker requires no special skill and can be done in a couple of hours. There are two pitfalls to avoid, however. First, if you are using copper supply tubing, bend it carefully, because one false move can cause an irreparable kink. Second, be sure to place the supply tube where it will be out of harm's way, especially when you pull out the refrigerator to clean the floor.

ATTACH A SADDLE TEE VALVE: Find a convenient location on a cold-water pipe. It should be near the refrigerator, up away from the reach of children, yet fairly easy to get to if you need to shut it off. The most common location is in the basement just below the refrigerator.

The puncture-type saddle tee is the easiest to install. There is no need to shut off the water. Just clamp the valve onto the pipe and turn the handle until it pokes through the pipe. However, this type clogs easily; use it only if you don't have any sediment in your water.

The other type, which is less likely to get stopped up, requires that you shut off the water and drill a hole in the pipe. Screw the valve into the hole and tighten the clamp.

RUN THE SUPPLY TUBING: Buy plenty of supply tubing, since it will probably not follow a straight path. Flexible copper tubing is preferable, but plastic line can be used.

Drill a hole at a location that will allow the supply tubing to run from the refrigerator to the saddle tee. Often it works best to drill a ¾-inch hole near the back wall or through the floor. If you need to drill through flooring and a finished ceiling below, use a long spade bit.

Working from the refrigerator space, gently uncoil the tubing. If you need to make a bend, make it as long

Drill a hole near the back of the refrigerator opening and thread the copper tubing down through it.

and sweeping as possible. Leave plenty of tubing in a coil in the refrigerator space, so you can pull out the refrigerator and push it back in without kinking.

CONNECT THE TUBING: Connect the tubing to the saddle tee, run water through the line to clear sediment, and then attach it to the refrigerator. The tubing must be inserted straight into the fittings. At each end, slip on a nut and a ferrule, slip the tubing into the fitting. Add pipe joint compound or Teflon tape to the male thread fittings and tighten the nut.

Saddle tee valve

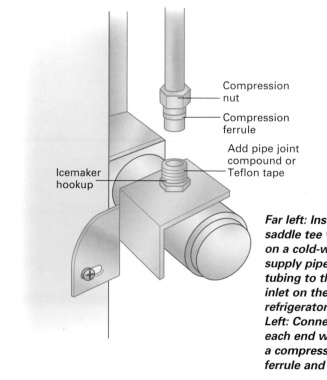

Compression nut

Compression ferrule

Add pipe joint compound or Teflon tape

Icemaker hookup

Far left: Install a saddle tee valve on a cold-water supply pipe. Run tubing to the inlet on the refrigerator. Left: Connect each end with a compression ferrule and nut.

WATER FILTERS

Water that comes from a public source should enter your house already treated (usually with chlorine) to eliminate harmful microorganisms and chemicals. Treating well water is up to the homeowner. If pesticides or industrial wastes are widely used in your area, or if you have any other reason to suspect that your water may be unsafe, contact your local health department, the municipal water supplier, an environmental conservation office, or an extension office of a local university to find the best way to test your water.

Water filters in the home are not designed to make unsafe water safe, but will make water better tasting, strain out particles that can damage appliances, and reduce minerals that leave stains and make it difficult to wash. In fact, a water filter may actually increase bacteria in your water by reducing chlorine.

For the types of filters and the problems they solve, see the chart on the next page. Most annoyances—bad taste, sediment, stains—can be solved with a water softener, sediment filter, and/or an activated-charcoal filter. The filter's packaging will tell you what problems it is designed to solve.

WHOLE-HOUSE FILTERS

You may want to install a whole-house sediment filter to reduce particles and an activated-charcoal filter under the sink to improve the taste of drinking water. Or, install both types side by side to serve the whole house. You will have to change whole-house charcoal filters more often than you

would with an under-sink unit, but you will know that water from every faucet will be purified.

LOCATION: Choose a place where you have a run of horizontal pipe and enough room for the unit. It should be easily accessible, because you will have to change filters every few months and inspect them even more often. Near the water meter is the most common location.

SHUT OFF THE WATER: Shut off the water prior to where you will be breaking in. Open a faucet at a low point in the house to drain the line as much as possible and place a bucket under the pipe to collect water that back drains.

CUT PIPE AND INSTALL FILTER: Open up a union, or cut into a pipe, and remove pipe as recommended by the manufacturer's instructions. Depending on your pipe, install nipples and unions or compression nuts and fittings. Make sure the filters are facing the right way.

GROUND WIRE: In many houses, the cold-water pipes are used to ground the electrical system. (You will see a thick bare wire emerging from the service panel and joining to a pipe via a clamp.) A filter (or a water meter) interrupts the path of the ground. It is very important that you clamp a jumper wire of the same thickness to both sides of the filters.

Some units have built-in shutoff valves located at the top, making it easy to stop the water in order to change cartridges. Mark your calendar for the recommended dates to change the filter.

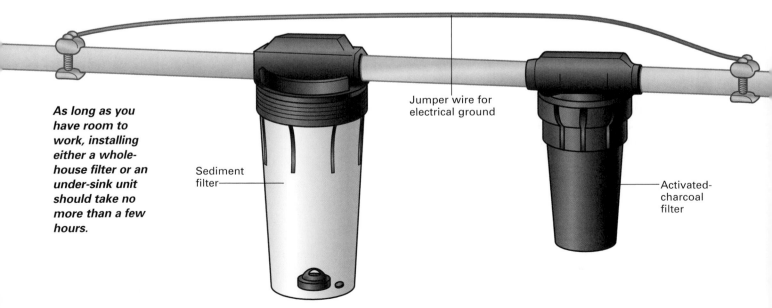

As long as you have room to work, installing either a whole-house filter or an under-sink unit should take no more than a few hours.

Sediment filter

Jumper wire for electrical ground

Activated-charcoal filter

UNDER-SINK FILTER

Most of your drinking water comes from the kitchen tap, so it makes sense to install a filter serving this fixture only. You can also install a separate faucet with the filter, much as you would a hot-water dispenser (*see page 80*). You may want to install a filter serving your icemaker as well (*see page 81*).

Most under-sink filters are designed to fit onto a solid chrome-plated riser. If you have a flexible riser (*see page 51*), you will probably need to buy another length of flexible riser and a tube union to connect the risers. Ask your plumbing supplier to equip you with all you need.

Anchor the filter at a spot where it can be easily reached for changing cartridges. Shut off the stop valve for the cold water and cut the riser with a tubing cutter. Connect the plastic supply lines with compression fittings. The filter is marked to tell you which is the inlet side and which is the outgo side.

Restore water pressure, and follow the manufacturer's directions for breaking in the system.

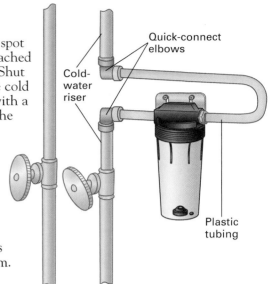

WATER SOFTENER

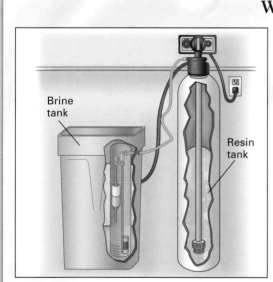

Hard water is one of the most common complaints about household water. Water that is laden with calcium, magnesium, iron, or other minerals will hamper lathering when used for washing. In addition, it will leave rings in tubs, and it can clog pipes and fixtures with mineral deposits. The best solution is a water softener.

A water softener must be filled with salt to function. Using a process called ion exchange, the softener removes minerals from the water and replaces them with sodium. As a result, softened water can clean well and will not harm your plumbing. But it also contains enough sodium to make the water taste bad. So if possible, have a cold-water line bypass the softener and supply unsoftened cold water for drinking.

To install a water softener, you will need to make drain, supply, and electrical connections, and will need to flush and recharge the system periodically. Often homeowners choose to rent a unit and let the supplier handle installation and maintenance.

WATER PROBLEMS AND SOLUTIONS

Problem	Solution
Reddish brown stains on bathtub and clothes.	A water softener will remove some iron. For water with heavy iron content, install an activated-charcoal (carbon) filter.
Water does not lather or wash well; white mineral deposits in faucets and showerheads.	Install a water softener.
Particles clog aerators and/or make water look cloudy.	Install a sediment filter.
Water tastes of chlorine, or tastes bad.	Install an activated-charcoal (carbon) filter under the kitchen sink.
You suspect the presence of bacteria or harmful chemicals.	Install a reverse-osmosis filter near the kitchen sink.
"Rotten egg" smell and taste due to the presence of sulfur (hydrogen sulfide).	A particle filter and an activated-charcoal (carbon) filter will help. For serious problems, install a chlorinization feeder system.

Installing new fixtures and appliances is not difficult. Make the job enjoyable with careful planning and layout. You'll be encouraged by the results of your well-planned efforts.

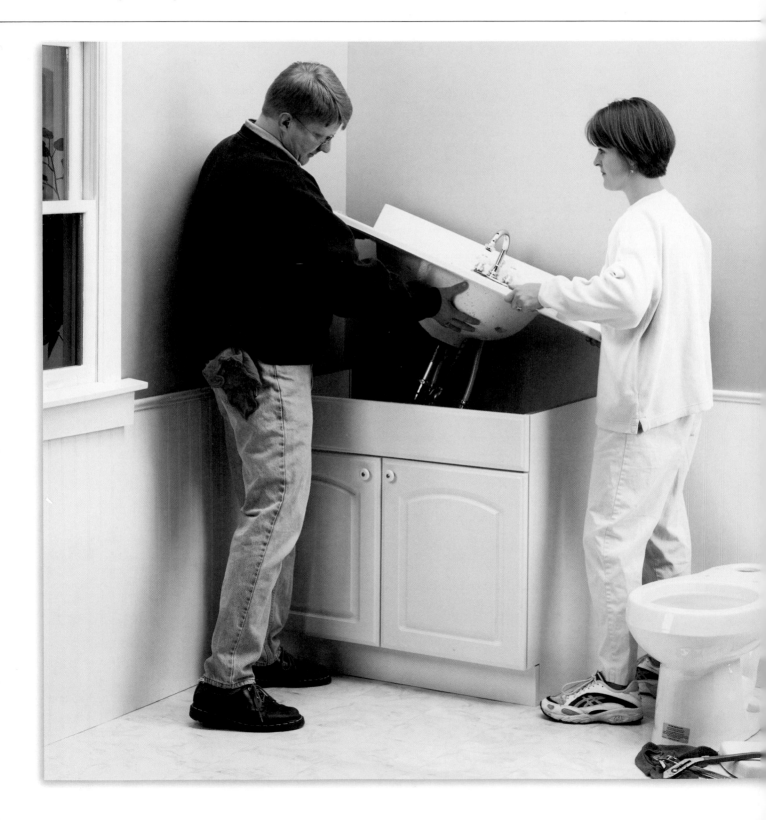

EXPANDING YOUR SERVICE

Adding supply and drain lines and installing new fixtures may appear to require much more work than plumbing repairs, but in some ways these projects are simpler. You'll be working with new materials, and if the installation requires remodeled floors and walls, access will be easier. Gone are the old fixtures; you'll be handling clean, new materials.

However, expanding your service will demand a sizable commitment of time and energy. The plumbing tasks described in the previous pages of this book can be accomplished in a couple of days or quicker—and with little disruption to your family. Those accomplishments provide excellent training for larger projects. Once you start running new lines and installing fixtures in new locations, you've entered the exciting realm of serious remodeling. Many a homeowner project that was supposed to take only a week or two has turned into a months-long nightmare. For the sake of your sanity and the well-being of the innocents who live with you, make a realistic appraisal of your abilities, and plan carefully.

Chances are, most of your time will be spent performing tasks other than plumbing. Floor and wall surfaces will need to be removed, then replaced after the plumbing is done; a new stud wall may need to be built; and tiling may be called for. Plan all phases of the job at the same time. Don't just tear into a wall or floor; remove it carefully so it will be easier to patch later.

Running pipes, tightening with wrenches, and soldering copper joints are difficult tasks to perform in cramped spaces. Often it is just as easy to remove and replace a large section of floor or wall as it is to cut out a small area. Give yourself plenty of room to work.

If possible, don't deprive your family of essential plumbing facilities. In fact, speed and convenience are often why homeowners hand these major installations to professionals. So your first challenge is to plan around any inconvenience. For example, if you will be removing the single toilet in the household, schedule the work so you can reinstall it the same day; if the kitchen sink is to be removed for a while, set up a temporary sink in the basement or another room.

PLANNING A NEW BATHROOM

Real estate agents say that a new or remodeled bathroom is often the only home improvement project that adds more value than it costs. If you do most of the work yourself, you come out even further ahead.

LOCATING THE PLUMBING

These minimum clearances are required by most codes. Check your local requirements. Measure and make a precise working plan of your project to avoid expensive surprises.

If you are willing to install new waste and vent pipes extending through the roof, you can put a new bathroom anywhere. However, this will mean tearing into walls, floors, and ceilings. Start by looking for an easier way: Find the main stack, called the soil stack or waste stack, which is located in a "wet wall." (*See the diagram on page 9.*)

Often the wet wall will be thicker than other walls. Toilets and other major fixtures are typically located near the main stack.

If there is an access panel behind a bathtub, open it and peer in with a flashlight. You may need to cut open part of a wall to be certain of the exact location of the stack.

Running supply lines is usually not nearly as difficult as running drain lines and vents. You can tie into hot and cold water lines at just about any point, and can run them in walls or floors in any direction.

As you are planning the location and arrangement of the fixtures, decide how you will tie into the stack in a way that satisfies venting requirements (*see pages 88–89*). Remember, also, that the stack must be securely supported above and below the cut.

STEALING SPACE

Unless you will be constructing an addition to your house, you will need to steal space for a new bathroom from existing floor area. Take measurements and draw a plan on graph paper to find out how much space can be taken for the new installation. Remember to take into account the thickness of any walls you will remove.

If you want to remove part of a wall, make sure it is not "load-bearing"—supporting an upper floor or the roof. If a wall runs parallel to the joists above, it is probably not load-bearing. A wall that is perpendicular to ceiling joists is not necessarily load-bearing, but one that has a wall directly above it is load bearing. Have a carpenter check it out if you are not sure.

ARRANGING THE FIXTURES

Because they are small, bathrooms call for careful placement of fixtures. Putting fixtures too close together can be inconvenient and may be in violation of local codes. The drawings *left* show the clearances required.

A toilet needs a minimum clearance of 15 inches on either side of its centerline and 48 inches of clear space from the wall. A door can swing into this space, and people can stand there when using other fixtures, but no fixed object can be in the way.

If possible, avoid squeezing in a small sink. A large sink or vanity top with space for toothbrushes and soap will make the bathroom more pleasant to use.

A standard bathtub is 32 inches wide and 60 inches (5 feet) long. A 54-inch tub will be noticeably smaller and less comfortable for bathing. Plan to cut out an access panel in the wall to make plumbing installation and later repairs easier. If you want to put in a large spa, plan its location first and design the rest of the bathroom around it.

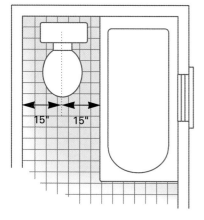

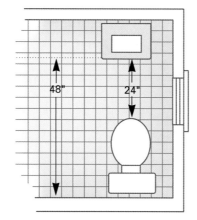

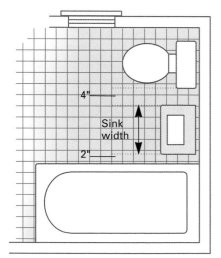

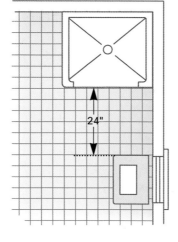

PLANNING THE ROUGH PLUMBING

Once you've located the stack, found the floor space, and decided on the locations of the fixtures, you're still not ready to start your demolition.

Experienced plumbers plan the exact locations all of pipes using pencil and paper:
■ Make a complete set of drawings, showing every wall where plumbing will be located.
■ Take the time to visualize where all the supply, vent, and drain lines will go.
■ Make sure the drain lines will slope properly and that the vents will be correctly positioned.
■ Try to imagine how you will install the plumbing, and leave enough clearance for using tools and soldering copper pipe.

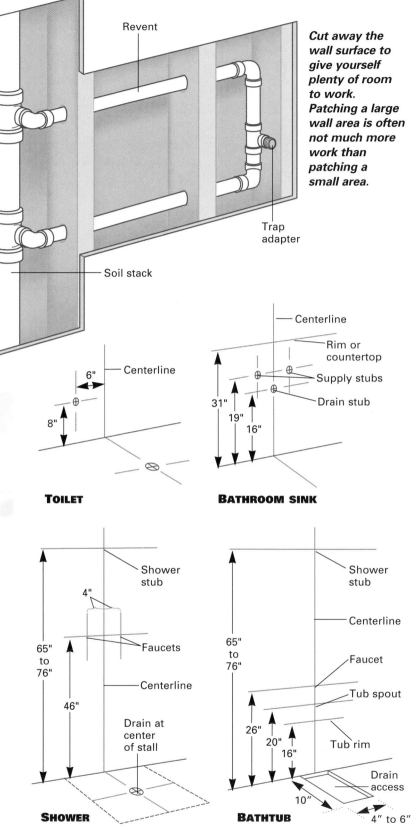

Cut away the wall surface to give yourself plenty of room to work. Patching a large wall area is often not much more work than patching a small area.

A TYPICAL SCHEDULE

Remodeling projects rarely go according to schedule, but it still pays to plan the order of work. This is the most likely sequence:
■ **DEMOLITION:** Tear out wall and floor surfaces so you can work easily. Mark and carefully store hardware, moldings, and other items that will be reused.
■ **ROUGH CARPENTRY:** Build any walls and frame openings for doors and windows.
■ **ROUGH PLUMBING:** Install and test all supply, drain, and vent lines.
■ **VENT:** Cut the hole and run a vent for the bathroom fan.
■ **BATHTUB:** Install the tub and shower faucet, and the bathtub or shower pad.
■ **ROUGH WIRING:** Run electrical cables and install any recessed fixtures and boxes.
■ **WALLBOARD AND SUBFLOOR:** Cover the walls with wallboard, tape, and paint with primer. Install plywood subflooring.
■ **TILING:** Install wall and floor tiles.
■ **PAINT:** Apply finish coat of paint.
■ **CABINETS:** Install vanity cabinet and any closets or other woodwork.
■ **FINISH PLUMBING:** Install sink, faucet, toilet, and the finish shower parts.
■ **TOUCH-UPS:** Don't be surprised to find lots of little fix-ups.

These are standard rough-in dimensions. Specially sized fixtures, such as whirlpools and odd-shaped shower stalls, will have different dimensions.

PLANNING VENTS

Without proper venting, water can drain sluggishly and gases can be released into the house. Vents are often the most difficult pipes to install, since they usually must be positioned higher than the drainpipes. That is why planning and installing rough plumbing always starts with the vents.

Sanitary cross

COMMON VENT

FOUR TYPES

When remodeling, there are four basic ways to vent a fixture. If there is an existing fixture with a trap tied to a vertical vent with a sanitary tee, you can connect your new fixture at the same place, by replacing the tee with a sanitary cross; this is called **common venting**, or unit venting. **Reventing**, or circuit venting, is very common in remodeling work. To revent, run a vent pipe up and over, and tie it to the stack at a higher point than an existing drain. **Separate venting**, running a new vent up and through the roof, may not be as difficult as it sounds if you are on an upper floor. **Wet venting** uses a section of another fixture's vertical drain line as a vent pipe. Many codes prohibit wet venting, or at least require that the vertical drain/vent be larger in diameter than the upper fixture drain.

REVENT

SEPARATE VENT

Sanitary Tee

Common venting, reventing, and separate venting are all widely accepted by local codes for a variety of situations. Wet venting is less commonly approved.

WET VENT

RULES FOR VENTS

The drain from every fixture must be connected to its own vent. The vent pipe from the fixture either extends directly through the roof or is connected to one that does. Following the rules described here will bring plumbing into compliance with most local building codes. Check with your building department for specific regulations. And check whether or not your municipality will let you tap into an existing vent; some require that only a licensed plumber do so.

DISTANCE FROM THE VERTICAL VENT:
Codes are specific about how far the trap outlet can be from the vertical vent. This will vary according to the size of the pipe, but in most cases a trap must be no farther than five feet from the stack serving as the vent.

SLOPE OF HORIZONTAL VENT PIPE:
A horizontal run of vent piping must slope ¼ inch per foot back to the drainpipe. This allows any waste that collects in the vent to drain out. Horizontal vent piping must be installed without low spots that could trap water and block the flow of air.

VENTING ABOVE FLOOD-RIM LEVEL:
The flood-rim level of a fixture is its overflow point—the level at which water begins to spill out onto the floor. Plumbing codes are careful to state that the horizontal member of a vent pipe must be at least 6 inches above the flooding level of a fixture. This elevation keeps drain water from a flooded fixture from flowing into another fixture through the vent. If the vents for two fixtures are connected together, both vents must be 6 inches above the flood-rim level of the higher fixture.

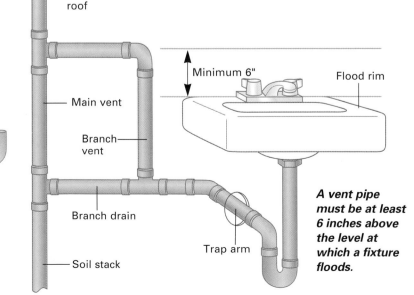

Vent to roof

Minimum 6"

Flood rim

Main vent

Branch vent

Branch drain

Trap arm

Soil stack

A vent pipe must be at least 6 inches above the level at which a fixture floods.

RULES FOR VERTICAL VENTING: The vent must always connect to the drainpipe at a point that will remain dry during normal usage. In addition, a vertical vent is always connected to the top of a horizontal drainpipe, so that passing waste water will not enter the vertical pipe.

RULES FOR HORIZONTAL VENTING: Any part of vent line that runs below the flood-rim level must be installed as if it were a drain line, using long-bend elbows and wyes, not sanitary tees or short-radius 90-degree bends.

RUNNING A SEPARATE VENT

Installing a new separate vent does not mean that you have to install a new drain as well; the drain line ties into an existing drain line. Use PVC for your new vent—it's light weight and makes cutting and installation easier.

Locate your vent line between studs and cut the top of the wall to give you access to the top plate. Use a hole saw to cut the hole for the vent pipe. Repeat this step at every story until you reach the attic.

Once you reach the attic, use a level or a plumb bob to find a spot in the ceiling directly above and drill a hole through the roof. From the outside, cut the shingles back and install a roof jack.

Have a helper shove a length of pipe through the roof jack while you guide it through the holes in the plates. If the run is over 10 feet (a standard pipe length), glue another pipe with a coupling and keep going. Glue the pipe at the tee at the bottom and patch your walls.

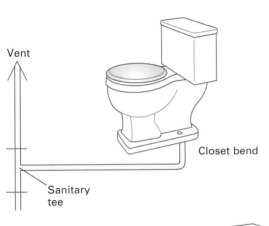

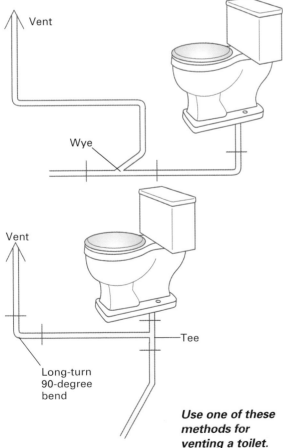

Use one of these methods for venting a toilet.

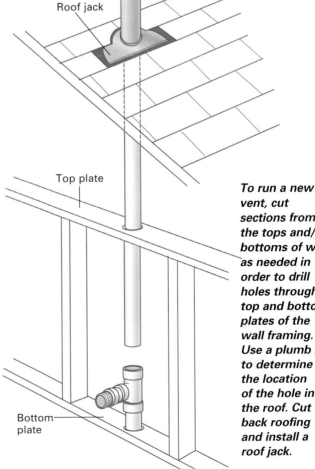

To run a new vent, cut sections from the tops and/or bottoms of walls as needed in order to drill holes through top and bottom plates of the wall framing. Use a plumb bob to determine the location of the hole in the roof. Cut back roofing and install a roof jack.

ROUGHING IN PIPES

Running new plumbing calls for spending a lot of time (probably more than you expected) in a small space. Take the time to make your job site well organized and safe.

MARKING AND CUTTING PATHWAYS FOR PIPES

Often it is easier in the long run to remove the surface from an entire wall rather than to cut sections of it: Not only will the plumbing be easier to install, with more room to move, but wallboarding an entire wall can be easier than patching small areas.

PRELIMINARY CUTOUTS: Measure and mark the subfloor for the cutout locations for the closet flange and the bathtub drain assembly (*see pages 87 and 93*). Drill ½-inch pilot holes and insert a wire to see if joists will be in the way. When possible, avoid cutting through joists by moving fixtures a few inches. For the toilet, cut a 5-inch hole for the closet flange. If you cannot install the trap and trap arm from underneath, cut the subfloor to give you access. Replace the access cut after you install the closet flange. For a bathtub, cut out an 8×10-inch area in the floor; this hole will remain after the tub is installed.

MARK STUDS, JOISTS, AND PLATES: Mark the locations of all holes and notches before you start drilling and notching. This will force you to figure out the exact paths the pipes will take and help you identify problem areas, such as where pipes must cross

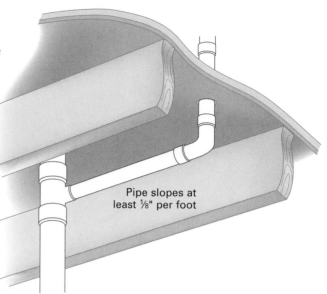

Pipe slopes at least ⅛" per foot

If the area below is a basement with an unfinished ceiling, running a new line will be comparatively easy.

each other. Remember to slope drain and vent pipes a minimum of ⅛ inch per foot and a maximum of ¼ inch per foot. In addition, keep these principles in mind:

■ Make joist holes as small as possible and leave at least 2 inches of wood intact at the bottom of each joist.

■ Where possible, run pipes beneath a joist. Avoid notching a joist; drilling a hole does not weaken it as much.

■ Do not drill holes in the middle third of a joist's span; this is where it bears the greatest load.

■ Where possible, drill holes in studs rather than notching them. You can drill out as much as two thirds of a stud width, as long as there is wood on either side of the hole. This allows room for a 2-inch, but not a 3-inch, pipe to run horizontally inside a standard 2×4 wall.

■ You can notch top and bottom plates, but if the notch extends into more than two thirds of the width of the plate, install a steel protector across the notch to stabilize it.

DRILLING AND CUTTING: Use a heavy-duty ½-inch drill and sharp bits. A right-angle drill is well worth renting, because it enables you to bore straight through studs and joists even when they are closely spaced. Have on hand a "cat's paw" nail remover and

Stubs

Slope toward tee

Sanitary tee

Tie into a drain line by cutting out a section of pipe and installing a sanitary tee. If the pipe is very rigid so that you cannot move one piece or other to slip in the tee, cut out a section and use a slip coupling. Be sure that the drain line slopes at least ¼ inch per running foot.

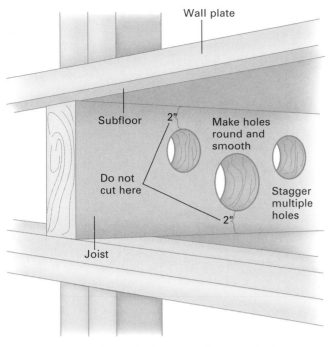

Wall plate

Subfloor

2"

Make holes round and smooth

Do not cut here

2"

Stagger multiple holes

Joist

Plan the location of holes carefully, especially where a drainpipe must slope. If you are forced to cut closer to the edge of a joist than recommended, reinforce the joist.

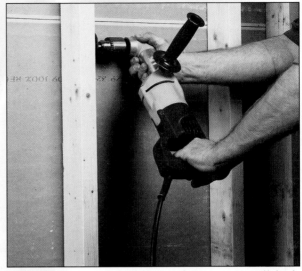

RIGHT-ANGLE DRILL

With studs or joists 16 inches or less apart, you'll find it difficult to bore neat holes for drain and vent pipes. A right-angle drill not only handles the job neatly, it will save you time. Most rental outlets stock it.

an old chisel. A reciprocating saw will save you lots of time and aggravation when you need to cut notches in tight places.

Don't drill through nail heads. Remove the nail or lop off the head with a chisel and use a nail set to drive the remainder of the nail through.

INSTALLING THE PIPES

Install the DWV pipes first; it's easier to run supply pipes around them than vice versa.
TEEING IN: Tie into a drain line by cutting the drainpipe and installing a tee (*opposite*), or by replacing a tee with a sanitary cross (*see page 88*). Use tees when tying into supply lines as well.
FITTING IN HORIZONTAL RUNS:
Sometimes it's impossible to thread long sections of pipe through studs, especially if the studs are closely spaced. You may be able to drill an extra hole at the end of a run to allow the pipe to be fed in from the outside; if not, cut the pipe into small lengths and couple it between studs.
DRY-FIT FIRST: Don't start gluing or soldering pipes until you are sure you have them correctly cut and aligned. Test your installation with a dry run. Apply flux to the copper pipes as you assemble them; that way,

you won't have to take them apart to solder. PVC pipes, however, must be dry-fit, marked for alignment, taken apart, primed, and glued.
FINISHING: Complete the rough-in by installing stubs that protrude into the room about six inches. Install stop valves, or temporarily cap supply-pipe ends if stop valves will get in the way of a cabinet installation; you can install the valves after the cabinet is in place.

Install clamps and test to see that the supply pipes are held firmly, so there will be no water hammer.

Test the system by turning the water back on and checking for leaks. An inspector may conduct a pressure test on the DWV pipes: With all the pipe ends capped off, air is pumped into the pipes and a gauge tells whether the pipes hold the pressure.

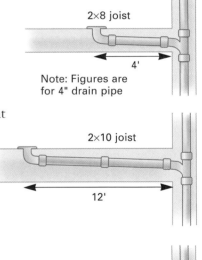

2×8 joist

4'

Note: Figures are for 4" drain pipe

2×10 joist

12'

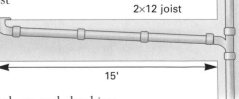

2×12 joist

15'

When you run drainpipes under a floor, consider slope. Wider joists allow longer drain runs.

ROUGHING IN A TUB/SHOWER

Plan the framing and plumbing for a tub and shower together, so you will have shower parts that are firmly affixed and accurately aligned.

A new tub and shower involves framing the walls, installing plumbing, and finishing the walls, perhaps with tile. Each step has to allow for the others, so plan the project completely before you start. For example, framing has to be positioned to make room for supplies and drains; plumbing has to be located to suit the thickness of the wall material, and the wall material has to be waterproof and shed water toward the drain.

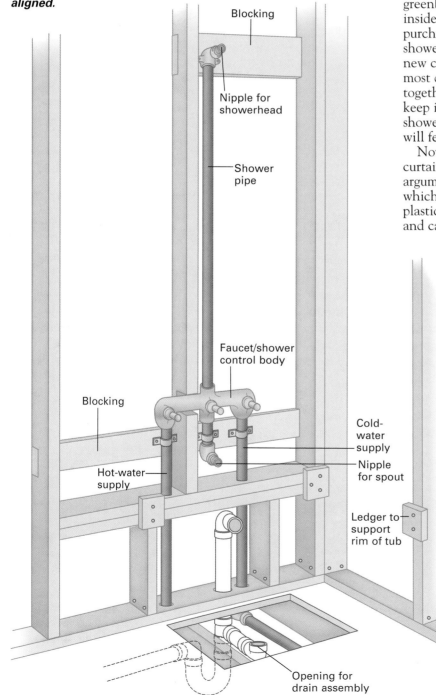

Blocking

Nipple for showerhead

Shower pipe

Faucet/shower control body

Blocking

Cold-water supply

Nipple for spout

Hot-water supply

Ledger to support rim of tub

Opening for drain assembly

TUB-AND-SHOWER OPTIONS

The most common tub-and-shower installation includes a 5-foot bathtub with three walls around it and a faucet located at one end. The walls should be covered with cement board if you plan to use ceramic tile and greenboard if you intend to finish the walls with sheets of fiberglass or plastic. Be sure that the tub has its drain hole in the correct place.

If you want a shower only, you can install a shower pad, build walls around it (most require three walls), and then install greenboard or cement board and tile on the insides of the walls. Or save time by purchasing a prefabricated fiberglass or vinyl shower stall. A one-piece unit is easiest in new construction, but is too big to fit through most doorways. Two- and three-piece stalls fit together easily. If you're building your own keep in mind that a 36-inch base makes for a shower that is comfortable to use; a 32-incher will feel crowded.

Now that water-repellent fabric shower curtains are available, there is no compelling argument for installing a glass shower door, which can be difficult to keep clean. Unlike plastic, fabric curtains rarely develop mildew and can be thrown in the washing machine.

INSTALLING THE FAUCET

A successful faucet installation is a marriage of carpentry and plumbing.

You'll need to install blocking for the faucet so it will be level, plumb, at the correct depth in the wall, and firmly anchored, and so that the handles, showerhead, and spout will be square to the wall and solid enough to withstand decades of tugging and turning.

Blocking for a tub spout typically is centered 4 inches above the top of the tub. For the showerhead, 6½ feet above the floor is a common height, but you may want it higher or lower. If the faucet will be more than 6 inches above the spout, install a third blocking piece just below the faucet, so the hot and cold pipes can be firmly clamped to solid lumber.

HOOK UP THE FAUCET: Read the manufacturer's instructions to find out how deeply in the wall the faucet should be placed.

Bathtub drain assembly

Take into account the thickness of the greenboard or cement board and the tile or sheeting that will be installed on top of it.

Run hot-water and cold-water supply lines (hot on the left, cold on the right) up to the location of the faucet. These must be installed precisely so that the faucet controls will be centered and level. The faucet will determine how far apart the supply pipes must be from each other. They must end at exactly the same height, and they must be placed so that the faucet will be centered from side to side. Recheck the depth of the faucet in the wall. You may need to insert some spacers to bring it out. Solder or compression-fit the faucet onto the supply lines.

Attach a drop ell to the top of the shower pipe and install it. Attach the ell to the blocking using galvanized screws. Install a nipple and a threaded ell for the spout. Clamp the pipes firm. Use galvanized nipples to stand in for the showerhead and spout. Place the handles on the faucet, turn the water on, and test for leaks.

INSTALLING THE DRAIN

Provide an access panel behind the tub. Cut a hole and use a piece of painted plywood with screws as the cover, or purchase a plastic plumber's access panel.

Buy a bathtub drain-overflow assembly and connect it to the tub before you move it into position. Hook up the drain (*see page 89 for venting*), but not the trap.

Slide the tub into position and anchor it according to the manufacturer's directions. In most cases, you will need ledger blocks of wood attached to the studs, to provide a resting place for the tub rim.

Once the tub is exactly where you want it, work from behind. Install the tailpiece onto the overflow assembly, and hook the P-trap to the drainpipe. Insert the tailpiece into the trap and tighten all the joints. To test the drain, fill the tub with water, lift up on the stopper, and look hard to find any drips.

INSTALLING A SHOWER STALL

Begin by roughing in a vented drain in the exact middle of the shower area. Set the base in place and hook up the drain. Test for leaks by pouring a 5-gallon bucket of water down the drain.

Frame the walls. Provide blocking and install a faucet much as you would for a tub and shower.

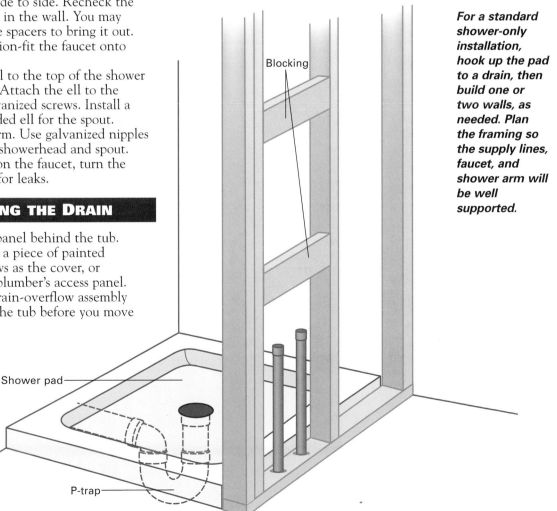

Blocking

Shower pad

P-trap

For a standard shower-only installation, hook up the pad to a drain, then build one or two walls, as needed. Plan the framing so the supply lines, faucet, and shower arm will be well supported.

INDEX